I Won't Die Hungry

A Holocaust Survivor's Memoir

Alice Singer-Genis
with Emunah Herzog

AuthorHouse™
1663 Liberty Drive
Bloomington, IN 47403
www.authorhouse.com
Phone: 1-800-839-8640

©2011 Alice Singer-Genis with Emunah Herzog. All rights reserved.

No part of this book may be reproduced, stored in a retrieval system, or transmitted by any means without the written permission of the author.

First published by AuthorHouse 4/29/2011

ISBN: 978-1-4567-3649-1 (sc)
ISBN: 978-1-4567-3650-7 (e)

Library of Congress Control Number: 2011901882

Printed in the United States of America

Any people depicted in stock imagery provided by Thinkstock are models, and such images are being used for illustrative purposes only.
Certain stock imagery © Thinkstock.

This book is printed on acid-free paper.

Because of the dynamic nature of the Internet, any web addresses or links contained in this book may have changed since publication and may no longer be valid. The views expressed in this work are solely those of the author and do not necessarily reflect the views of the publisher, and the publisher hereby disclaims any responsibility for them.

Dedicated to my grandchildren

Ryan, Brittany, Isaiah, and Mariah.

Foreword

When Alan Adelson from Jewish Heritage in New York approached me about assisting a Holocaust survivor in writing her memoir, I knew immediately what an honor this was. I also knew that I would learn much in the process. What I didn't know was how enjoyable working with Alice would be, and what a wonderful friendship would ensue from this collaboration.

Alice Singer-Genis is a most remarkable woman. Still beautiful and elegant despite her age, often a light smile on her face, Alice is as much a lady as she describes her mother as being throughout the book. Again and again, it amazed me that after hours of revisiting experiences ranging from challenging to horrific, I would not walk out of Alice's house heavy-hearted. Instead, after a warm hug goodbye, I'd feel a spring in my step, looking forward to working on what we had discussed.

Alice has the unusual ability to detach without closing her heart; to tell the truth clearly, yet in an understated way that penetrates deeply; and to see the strength of the human spirit where others might focus on the darkness of the human condition. Her sense of humor and appreciation for beauty never faltered, despite the many difficult circumstances throughout her entire life.

I was born and raised in Germany and converted to Judaism after immigrating to Canada as a young adult. The Holocaust has been a central theme in my life which made working with Alice especially meaningful. I am filled with immense gratitude for having participated in documenting this incredible woman's extraordinary story for many generations to come. Their lives will be changed by reading this story, as was mine in helping Alice to write it.

Emunah Herzog, November 14, 2010

Chapter One

ONE OF MY EARLIEST MEMORIES – it would have been in the late 1920s because I was born in 1926 – is feeling the warmth and shelter of my father's arms as he carried me up the stairs from my grandparents' apartment to ours after a Passover Seder. Our large extended family lived in a beautiful house in Vilno, overlooking the Vilia River. My sister still occasionally reminds me how, when we left in 1939, lugging as much as we could take on the train with us, I talked to the house.

"Good bye, house," I said. "I hope to see you again."

But let me not get ahead of myself.

In the early 1920s, my grandfather, Irma Singer, and his brother, Lipa Singer, bought a mansion which had been converted from a castle – originally built by a count – into an apartment building.

The city of Vilno has a long and complicated history. It was under Lithuanian, Polish, German, and Russian reign at different times over the centuries. Today it is once again the Lithuanian capital and is called Vilnius. The city first appeared in written sources in 1323, in letters by the Grand Duke Gediminas to German cities, inviting Germans as well as members of the Jewish community to settle in the then capital of Lithuania. His grandson, Prince Jagiello, married the young Polish Queen Jadwiga and, at that time, Poland united with Lithuania. In 1386 Jagiello became King of Poland and Grand Prince of Lithuania and continued to invite Jews to Vilno.

During the years my family lived in Vilno, the city belonged to Poland. The predominant language was Polish, and Yiddish, to a lesser extent. We spoke mostly Polish, my grandparents spoke Yiddish, and the older generation knew Russian.

Alice Singer-Genis with Emunah Herzog

My grandfather, his brother, and their families lived in this house. My father, Nochem, had three sisters and two brothers. My grandfather's brother had four sons, one of them married. Every family had their own apartment. So the whole Singer clan lived in this big, magnificent house. Even though other tenants resided in the building as well, it was commonly called "the Singer House."

My grandparents lived on the second floor and my grandfather's brother and his wife on the ground floor. All apartments were lovely, but theirs were the most beautiful. Both had a big salon, with huge, rounded windows, built into the tower of the original castle. I remember especially my grandparents' apartment, because I spent a lot of time there. The garden was very pretty. In the spring the smell of the lilac trees was everywhere, and there were yellow acacias and white jasmine and many other flowers. In the fall, my grandfather had a Sukkah[1] in the garden.

My father and grandfather were lumber merchants. My grandfather was traditional and supported the Chasidim[2] and a Yeshiva[3], but he was also modern and only had a small beard. My father was really a man of the world, not so traditional. But we kept a kosher home. My mother lit the candles on Friday nights but at the same time she was liberal.

My mother was born Miriam Schmidt in Smarhon, a small town between Vilno and Minsk. During WWI, as a child, she experienced the war directly. The fighting, the so-called front, was in her town. At that time, my mother's family had been divided already. Her father, her two brothers, and two of her sisters had left before the war for America. When they left, my mother, the youngest of the children, was just a little girl. So she stayed behind, together with her mother and my mother's older married sister with her husband, daughter, and son. The fighting got so bad that they had to flee from home. They ended up as refugees, very poor, in Kharkov, in the Ukraine.

The refugees had a difficult life. My mother wanted to go to school, to the Gymnasium, which in America would be called high school, except the Gymnasium was a high school that prepared the students to go to university. But she didn't have the money to pay for tuition. She wrote a letter to the Czar's daughter, Princess Tatiana, telling her that she was a

---

1 An outside hut where meals are eaten during the Jewish holiday of Sukkot (fall harvest)
2 A branch of Orthodox Judaism that promotes joy and spirituality
3 A religious Jewish school

refugee and couldn't afford schooling. Fortunately, the Princess granted my mother permission to attend the Gymnasium free of tuition.

My mother spent the remaining war years in Kharkov. She lived through the revolution. After the war and the revolution ended, she came with her mother back to Vilno. Finally, after all those difficult years, they received papers to go to America from her father.

My mother's mother was related to my father's mother. I believe they were second cousins. My mother's mother decided to visit my father's family before they left for America. This is how my mother met my father.

They fell in love right away. My father proposed marriage and she accepted. But my grandfather had different plans for his son. In those days, most marriages were still arranged and my grandfather wanted my father to marry a girl from Riga, from a rich, respected family. He didn't want him to marry a poor refugee. Mother told me that Father didn't fight with his father, but was diplomatic and finally got my grandfather to agree. So she decided to stay in Vilno. They had a big wedding where not only the rich invited guests were welcomed, but also the poorest Jews got to celebrate and eat well. No one was turned away. This was a custom of the Chasidim and my grandfather was happy to do it.

Soon after the wedding, my mother's mother left for America to join her husband and her other children. My mother's older sister stayed in her hometown, Smarhon, for a while, and soon went with her husband to Palestine, leaving her youngest daughter Miriam with my mother. The young girl still attended the Gymnasium and wanted to finish her schooling, so she lived with us. She had the same name as my mother, and everybody called them Mira. When they needed to clarify, they'd say "big Mira" and "little Mira," just like I was "big Asya" and Aunt Ella's daughter was "little Asya." (I only became Alice when people in America didn't pronounce my name properly.)

My childhood was very happy. My sister Edith and I – Edith is three years my junior – had loving parents and we enjoyed living with our large extended family in the beautiful house near the river. During the warmer months we played ball in our courtyard. In the winter we went sled riding on a hill that was part of our property.

When I was very young I had a nanny; I only remember her from a photograph. Later I had a governess. She was a student from Warsaw, and then, Mrs. Losofska lived with us although I don't remember what brought her to our home. Her daughter was my first piano teacher.

Mrs. Losofska was very strict. She got up early in the morning when Mother still slept. I remember having tea from a big Samovar[4]. I looked at that Samovar while Mrs. Losofska braided my hair, very, very tight; it actually hurt. She supervised my piano practice and my homework, and she had an important influence on me. I understand she and her daughter later went to Ponary from the Vilno Ghetto and perished there.

Aside from our home in Vilno, my family had several other investments, such as a lumber mill in Voropaevo. They built a glass factory there as well. We went to Voropaevo for the summers when I was a little girl. My sister and I had a puppy there. He had such soft fur and we loved to play with him. One day he was run over by a horse and buggy, which was the main form of transportation in those days. Edith and I were heartbroken, so the two of us buried the little dog and held a funeral for him.

Unfortunately my family's business luck changed. There was a so-called crisis in the country, like the Depression in the USA. The lumber mill burned down and the glass factory was in trouble. My family lost everything they owned, including the big house in Vilno. My grandfather never recovered from the loss. He was an honorable and proud man and had always been charitable, helping people wherever he could. His word was as good as money. He and my grandmother moved to Gleboki, where they had a married daughter, my Aunt Hannah.

However, Father started a business on his own, again as a lumber merchant. He worked hard, was able to rent our apartment, and his business did well. So we continued to live in the Singer House, even though our family didn't own it anymore. Consequently, my life didn't change much.

I went to good schools. During primary school, I began learning to play the piano and later, when I went to the Gymnasium, I took piano lessons with an excellent teacher who was a professor at the Jewish conservatory for music. I've loved music since I was a young girl and still do. Vilno was known for its intelligentsia and culture, and the Jewish conservatory for music was famous. So were schools and libraries and

---

4 A metal container traditionally used to heat water for tea in Eastern European countries and in the Middle-East

the theater. The YIVO, which is based in New York today and formally known as the YIVO Institute for Jewish Research, was founded in Vilno as the Yiddish Scientific Institute ("Yidisher Visnshaftlekher Institut.") Mother took me to the "Operetta" – Polish musical theater of high quality.

Our house was always filled with people. After my grandparents left, Father's youngest sister Celia still lived in her lovely room with a balcony, but she was alone, so Mother invited her to dine with us. Another uncle, Uncle Hirshl, stopped in regularly, and some of the people who worked for us came for dinner. Father had many business contacts. Mother volunteered at the orphanage. Once a week on Shabbat, a boy from the orphanage came to eat with us. Mother was a very pretty, elegant woman and had interesting friends, both women and men. There were always engaging discussions at our dinner table. From literature to music to politics, everything was covered. It was a good home to grow up in. I learned a lot listening to the adults.

My Uncle Hirshl was an ardent Beitarist, a follower of Jabotinsky, a very conservative Zionist. Uncle Hirshl wanted to go to Palestine to fight. But my grandfather wouldn't let him. My grandfather wanted to keep the family together. Today Uncle Hirshl's son, Aryeh, lives in Israel. He fought in the Israeli army and is a retired colonel. Cousin Mira was in favor of the Labor Zionist Party. Uncle Hirshl and Mira didn't agree. Mother was always liberal. Father was always for democracy and continued being charitable and generous. Every week they discussed current events and were always on top of what was going on. I remember how these conversations grew more and more serious after Hitler came to power in Germany.

In the 1930s, Mother went back to school and soon graduated as a nurse. In Vilno, there was a good nursing school, connected to the Jewish hospital.

After graduating from the Gymnasium, my cousin, Mira, went to the Stefan Batory University in Vilno, a prestigious school, one of the oldest in the region. However, the situation there was unpleasant. The anti-Semitic students wanted the Jewish students to sit only on the left side of the auditorium. The Jewish students protested and decided to stand during the lectures. After one year, Mira quit the university and went to nursing school instead. When she became a nurse, she followed her family to Palestine.

Ever since the lumber mill had burned down in Voropaevo, we spent the summers in Podbrodzie, where we rented a "Dacha", a summer house, in the woods. We had a veranda overlooking the forest. The kitchen was separate from the house. Our maid came with us from the city. She cooked in the kitchen and served our meals on the veranda. In front of the house was a hammock between the trees. I loved lying in the hammock, listening to birdsong and watching the sunrays sparkle through the leafy roof above me. Not too far from us was a river where the summer people went swimming and kayaking.

When I was twelve years old in Podbrodzie, I met a boy who was my first puppy love. We swam in the river and went for long walks in the woods and talked a lot. I'll always remember that summer. I was so happy! Never again would I feel the security I had as a child.

I Won't Die Hungry

My parents wedding with all my aunts and uncles at our family house.
Vilno, Poland (1924)

Alice Singer-Genis with Emunah Herzog

A family portrait of my mother, father, younger sister Edith and me.
Vilno, Poland (Late 1920's)

Partial View of our house. My grandparent's apartment was on the second floor and my Uncle Lipa's apartment was on the ground floor. Our apartment is not visible from this angle.
Vilno, Poland

Alice Singer-Genis with Emunah Herzog

Me with my mother.
Vilno, Poland (1927)

I Won't Die Hungry

My older cousin Mira standing next to me on a sled.
Vilno, Poland (Late 1920's)

Alice Singer-Genis with Emunah Herzog

Edith, Mother and I in
front of our house.
Vilno, Poland
(Early 1930's)

Mother, Father, Edith and I.
Vilno, Poland (1939)

Chapter Two

Like the year before, we spent the summer of 1939 in Podbrodzie. I had stayed in touch with my puppy love, but this year he and his family didn't come to the countryside.

In September of 1939, the war began. Father was away on business. Cousin Mira, who had come for a visit from Palestine, was staying with us. As soon as we heard the news, we tried to get back home to Vilno. Mother, Mira, Edith, our maid, and I packed our belongings as quickly as we could and went to the train station. But when we got there, no trains were available. We were told that they had been taken by the army.

Thousands of summertime vacationing people, like my family, waited with bundles. After hours of waiting, a boy we knew who was in the army put us on a freight train, and together with the soldiers, we finally got back to Vilno.

Mira's fiancé, Sima, a medical student, who had almost completed his studies and who was part of the reason Mira had returned to Poland from Palestine, was drafted into the army right away. A few days later the Germans started bombing Vilno.

"It's too dangerous in the city," Father said. "We have to go to the country until things calm down." He decided we would go to Gleboki, a small town northeast of Vilno, where his parents and his unmarried brother, Mula, lived, as well as his oldest sister Hannah with her husband, Uncle Moshe, and their two sons. Mira helped us pack. Father tried to convince her to go back to Palestine immediately, but she didn't want to leave her fiancé behind, so she stayed in Vilno. Both Mira and her fiancé, Sima, would be held in several concentration camps in the coming years.

It was very, very hard for us to leave our home in Vilno, even though we had no idea of the horrific years that lay ahead of us. Expecting to return soon, we left our furniture, crystal, and almost everything else behind. We took only our clothes and our valuables, like the silver, and whatever we could pack and take by train with us. But somehow we must have sensed that this was going to be more than a temporary absence, because it was then that my sister heard me talk to the house on the way down the stairs. She was ten years old, and I was thirteen.

"Good bye, house. I hope to see you again."

Our family never returned. Not until over fifty years later, in October of 1994, when Edith and I visited Vilno – which had become Vilnius – did I see the house again.

My parents rented a small, very modest house in Gleboki. How we missed Vilno! I missed my beautiful apartment, the spacious and cheerful room I had shared with my sister, the bathroom with a tub and hot water, and the telephone. We didn't have any of these conveniences here. Instead, we had to go to an outhouse. I never knew such a thing existed. Little did I know that compared to what was to come, this was still luxurious.

Only two weeks later, Poland was defeated and divided between Germany and the Soviet Union. Gleboki became part of the Belarusian Republic which was part of the Soviet Union. Vilno was also taken over by the Soviets, but at this point was given to Lithuania. We had to make a decision between going back to Vilno, Lithuania, or staying in Gleboki in the Soviet Union.

I wanted to go back to Vilno so badly, and I know Mother also missed our life in Vilno terribly – but my parents decided to stay in Gleboki. Aunt Celia lived with her parents and Uncle Mula now. As far as I remember, Uncle Hirshl and his family had stayed in Vilno, as had Uncle Lipa, my grandfather's brother, and his family. I believe Aunt Ella and little Asya were with our part of the Singer clan in Gleboki, but I don't remember if they lived with Aunt Hannah and Uncle Moshe or with my grandparents. By this time, Aunt Hannah's sons, Niunka and Elusha, had gone to Lvov, a beautiful city in Western Ukraine. Niunka attended the Polytechnicum and was close to graduating as an engineer, and Elusha began studying law.

As soon as the schools reopened, Edith and I continued our education. The Polish Gymnasium was changed into a Russian "Desiatiletka", a ten-year school, which is where I went. Edith was still in primary school.

Mother got a job as a nurse in a clinic. Father had to apply for work in another town where people didn't know him. In Gleboki, he was known to be a wealthy man, so he wasn't able to get a job. Being a lumber specialist, he found employment in Lyntupy, which was quite far away, especially since transportation wasn't what it is today. He only came home every few weeks.

Life in the Soviet Union was different. In the beginning it was happy. There was a lot of singing and dancing. I learned Russian quickly and soon spoke it fluently. People told me that I sounded like a native. I liked Russian literature and history was my favorite subject. We still had some old teachers from before the war, and some new ones came from the Soviet Union. As always, I enjoyed school and luckily I made many friends. Gleboki had a large Jewish population, and there were several Jewish children in my class.

The winter of 1939/40 was bitterly cold. Fortunately, our little house was warm. Outside, however, a fierce wind blew, and even though I wore heavy clothes, I was still cold – especially when I walked over a frozen lake every day to school and back. But it was much shorter than to walk all the way around so, together with a Russian girl named Vera, I took the shortcut across the icy surface.

One day, we saw a boy walking in the same direction ahead of us. He was tall, blond, and very handsome. I knew him from school – he was actually in my class – but I had never talked with him. Vera was a couple of years older than we were. She called out to the boy.

"Hey, Comrade Handsome!"

She turned to me. "I think this is the right boy for you," she said.

"Comrade Handsome, stop! Comrade Handsome, wait for us!" she kept yelling across the frozen lake.

Finally the boy stopped and we caught up with him. He blushed – we were so young, only fourteen years old – but soon we were engaged in a lively conversation. That was how I met Bomka. Of course I had no idea what an important role he would play in my life.

Bomka Genichowicz was born in Plissa, a tiny town in Eastern Poland. His mother came from Viennese Jews. His father owned a turpentine factory. Bomka's mother stayed home – like most women did at that time – and took care of Bomka and his younger brother, Borka (Boris.) So Bomka spent his early childhood in a rural environment, ice-skating in the winter and swimming and horseback riding in the summer. Plissa only had an elementary school, and when Bomka graduated his parents enrolled him in the Hebrew Gymnasium, "Tarbut", in Vilno. Here Bomka lived with a family whose sons attended the same excellent school. Everything was taught in Hebrew and the boys studied English as a second language. In his free time, Bomka went ice-skating and joined a Zionist Youth Organization. Because of the war, he had to leave Vilno and his parents arranged for him to live with another family in Gleboki so he could continue a good education.

From the day we met, Bomka and I spent much time together. When we went out with a group of friends, we always walked and talked just the two of us. Everybody saw us as a couple. Bomka was well liked everywhere. He came to my house often. My family immediately took a liking to him, and even our housekeeper, Wara – we were allowed to have a housekeeper because Mother worked – was friendly to him. Wara never smiled at any of my other friends, but when she saw Bomka, her face lit up. In school, too, the students and teachers were fond of him. He was elected to be class president, and I was vice president. When spring came, the bitter cold was forgotten. Everything was blooming and it was beautiful.

But life didn't remain cheerful in the Soviet Union. More and more often, we heard of people being arrested and many families were deported at night. We didn't know where they were taken. Pretty soon Lithuania, Latvia, and Estonia were incorporated into the Soviet Union as three new republics. There was fighting close to us in Finland. We only heard how well the Soviet Army did. Many years later when I was in Finland, I heard a different story: how hard the Fins fought for their country, and how proud they were of holding back the Soviet attack.

The following school year, Bomka did not return to Gleboki and I didn't see him anymore. In early 1941, my parents decided it would be best for us to move to Svencionys, which belonged to Lithuania and was only twelve kilometers from Lyntupy where Father worked.

Once again, my parents rented a small house. Mother got a job at the Department of Health. Father still couldn't come home every night, but we saw more of him than when we lived in Gleboki. Edith and I had to go through new beginnings in yet another school. Because many of the children in Svencionys had gone to a Jewish primary school and had lost a year, I was now in a class where everyone was at least a year older than I. And because I arrived in the middle of the term, groups and cliques had formed already, and I felt like an outsider. But a Soviet-Russian girl, Lydia, who was also new to the school, became friendly with me. Not much later I also got to know her older brother, Andrei.

And this is how I met Andrei: I loved history. My history teacher, who was the principal of the school, put me in charge of the historic society. I went to the higher grades to mobilize students to join our history group. Andrei, my friend Lydia's brother, became interested not only in the historic society, but also in me.

We went for long walks in the evenings. Spring was here and it was beautiful. We had much in common and liked many of the same things. Andrei said a lot was wrong with the Soviet Union, but he was a patriot and loved his country. He was tall, dark, and handsome, energetic and intelligent. But I never invited him to my house.

The school year went by quickly. After it ended, the school hired a bus, and we went on an outing to a lake near Svencionys. I remember it was a warm, sunny day when we heard someone say, "The Germans attacked us."

"That's impossible," my friend Lydia said. "We have a treaty of non-aggression with Germany."

We continued our trip as planned and went boating. I sat in a boat with Andrei. I remember him saying, "Hitler is an anti-Semite, but we will take care of you. Nothing will happen to you."

Within a few short days, all Soviet people left to escape the approaching German army. Lydia, Andrei, and their family too returned to the Soviet Union. We were left behind to face the music.

After the liberation, Father went to Svencionys. He brought me a postcard from Andrei, sent to the City Hall, asking about what happened to me. On the postcard was only a military number. I wrote back to this number, but never received an answer.

The Soviet army retreated quickly. The Germans moved ahead even quicker. Many Soviet soldiers surrendered. The Lithuanians organized a Nazi police force and the pro-Nazi element took over right away. Our maid left immediately. Edith and I helped Mother get the housework done. I remember doing a lot of ironing, which I enjoyed much more than some of the other chores. As always my family pulled together.

One day, the bus driver who had taken us on the outing to the lake showed up at my house. He was a young guy and at first I didn't even recognize who he was.

"So where are your friends now?" he said.

I told him they'd gone back to the Soviet Union.

"It's going to be very bad for the Jews," he said.

I got angry with him because I didn't understand why he was trying to scare me. What could I do about it, anyhow? Only later did I realize that he actually had come to warn me.

Soon after the Germans took over, a Lithuanian policeman, led by a Lithuanian man whom we didn't know, came to our house. He pointed at Father and said to the policeman, "This is a communist. Arrest him."

The policeman pulled out his gun and took Father with him. We didn't know what happened to our beloved father. We were sure they were going to shoot him. Several days went by in sheer agony. Mother couldn't get any information about his whereabouts, and we began to lose hope, becoming more and more certain that he had been killed. We were overwhelmed with grief and cried all the time, desperate, not knowing what to do.

And then, suddenly, there he was, walking through the door. Our bitter tears of sadness turned into sweet tears of joy. It felt like a miracle, like he had come back from the dead. Between hugs and kisses, he told us what had happened.

The Lithuanian policeman had taken him directly to jail. The prisoners were told that shortly the Germans would take over the command of the prison. When the German Chief arrived, he inspected every single prisoner and asked why he was in jail. When it was Father's turn, he said, "I don't know why I was arrested. Someone accused me of being a communist."

The German Chief asked him, "Are you a communist?"

"No," Father said.

Then the German looked him over and said, "This man is not a communist."

So the German Chief let Father go free and there he was, back home with us. I cannot describe how happy we were. I still feel that was one of the many miracles that happened to us.

Some time in the summer of 1941, Father heard a rumor that the Jews of Svencionys were going to be deported. Right away Father made a plan. He and a few men who worked with him in Lyntupy, Belarus, would walk to Lyntupy. The men would leave in the morning. The women and children would follow by horse and wagon in the darkness of night.

In the evening Mother told us to put on as much clothing as we could. I managed to get into six dresses. Edith did the same. Mother handed me some money. "Put it in your purse, Asya," she said, "and take good care of it."

This time we couldn't take any luggage with us. We just walked out at night in the dark. Father had arranged for a Polish man with horse and buggy to take us and Mother's two cousins – all of us women and children – across the border to Belarus.

As fate wanted it, once the coachman got into the woods, he made a wrong turn and got lost. He drove us around in circles until suddenly we were stopped by the Lithuanian police. We were all terrified. Mother panicked and tore up the papers she had taken, such as her diploma, Father's business contracts, and other documents.

One of the policemen made a big fuss about the torn papers, accusing us of being Russian spies who were taking papers to the enemy. Needless to say, anybody could see that a group of women and children were no spies. After much yelling and cursing they took us to the police station. They also hit the Polish man for driving Jews, but then they let him go. We'll never know if it was a coincidence or if he got lost on purpose so we would get caught. They commanded us to walk without telling us where we were going.

Once we arrived at the police station, everybody was searched. A policeman told me to give him everything I had. Quickly, I gave him my purse with the money. Then I took my earrings out of my ears and my ring off my finger and handed everything over to him. Next, I took all my dresses off, except the one closest to my skin. Only later did I have time to think about how much I liked the small, golden earrings that had been put in my ears when I was a baby – I never took them off – and the little ring with a ruby that my grandfather had given me for my birthday. Everybody obeyed as I did; we were very scared. However, Luba, one of

Mother's cousins, had covered some gold with material and sown it as buttons onto her blouse. They cut off the buttons, and the gold showed. They screamed at her, and beat her, and made sure that she gave over everything she had too.

After they confiscated our valuables, they made us walk through a long, long corridor. It was absolutely terrifying. They shouted at us to march in twos. Both Edith and I wanted to go with our mother, but Edith was quicker and grabbed Mother's hand before I did. So I went with Mother's cousin. I think that was the first time I was truly afraid for my life. The corridor seemed to go on forever and we were sure they were taking us outside to shoot us.

But they didn't. Not yet, anyway. Instead, they shoved us into a cell. There was a young woman in the cell when we came in. I remember talking with her. She was accused of being a communist. All night we waited to be taken out and shot. Every time we heard steps outside the prison cell, we thought, "This is it. Now they're coming to kill us." No one slept a wink. The tension and fear we felt during this long, dark night is indescribable.

In the morning, they came to the cell and took us out. The woman I talked with was left behind. Again we thought they were going to shoot us, but instead they marched us to the town square. In the square were many, many people and more arrived all the time. It looked like the whole Jewish population of Svencionys was there. Mother's other cousin, Chaya-Sorel, went to the outhouse close to the square and escaped. I'm sad to say that in the end she didn't survive though.

The rest of us stayed in the town square of Svencionys together with countless other Jews, all day long. Finally, the policemen ordered everybody to march on the road. We didn't know where we were going. A crowd of thousands of people was pushed by the Lithuanian police on horses. Old, young, sick, healthy, everybody was marching while the policemen yelled, cursed, and beat people on both sides of the crowd. We tried to walk in the middle so as not to be beaten.

After hours of this horrendous march we arrived at several barracks in the woods. Before we were allowed to go inside, out of cruelty, they had us jump over a fire. Then, men, women, children, old and young, were shoved into the barracks like cattle.

This place was called Poligon.

Chapter Three

THE TIME IN POLIGON WAS the absolute worst time of my life. For much of my life, I've blocked out what happened there. I just didn't want to think about it. Even now as I'm trying to remember, I can't access many of the details that must be stored somewhere in my brain.

I think it was in Poligon when I really woke up to the reality of how evil people can be, how much they can hate. How much they hated us. Up until then, I was so naïve. You see, I grew up in a very warm home, surrounded by good people who cared about each other. My grandparents and my parents had always been charitable and I simply did not know hate. So the reality in Poligon was entirely strange and unexpected, a devastating shock for me. But let me try to recount what I do remember.

I was always hungry.

Jews were brought to Poligon from many surrounding towns. The camp was supervised by a Lithuanian commandant and Lithuanian police. They must have been under German command, but we didn't see any Germans at first.

The barracks were terribly overcrowded. Somehow we inmates organized ourselves. We ended up sleeping in a barrack for the medical staff, because Mother was a nurse. The doctors and their families stayed there, along with the nurses and other people who had worked in the hospital in Svencionys. It was very stuffy and crowded inside the barrack. We spent much of the time outside. We were always hungry and always waiting to be sent to work somewhere. Waiting and being hungry, being hungry and waiting. Edith cried a lot and was very afraid. For some reason, even in those conditions, I didn't think we were going to be killed. What I remember most is how hungry I was all the time. I don't remember what they gave us to eat at all, don't remember where we went to the bathroom, how we kept ourselves clean. As I said, there's a part of me that has entirely blocked out this time.

One day some high rank German officers came. That was the first time I saw the insignia on the German soldiers' belts: "Gott mit uns – God with us." They ordered everybody to come out from the barracks and to form a column. We stood in formation and waited for what was to come next. Edith was crying and holding on to Mother.

"They're going to kill us," Edith said.

I could not believe they would kill us. After I don't know how long of us standing there, they let us go. Back to the barracks we went. But it was a rehearsal of what was to come. We began hearing the word "extermination."

There was a moment of humanity in this hell. One day when I was standing outside the barrack, a young policeman started to talk with me. We talked about different things. I soon forgot about it. That night somebody knocked at the door of our barrack. We were very frightened. Someone opened the door.

A policeman stood in front of our barrack. "Where is the blond girl?" he asked.

The people said, "There is no blond girl here."

But the young policeman insisted and didn't want to leave. Finally I came to the door. He handed me a loaf of bread and walked away.

Over the next few days, we noticed that some families were called and left the camp. Mother knew the man who arranged it. He was an electrician, a Jewish man, from Podbrodzie, where we used to go for the summer. He remembered us.

"If you have any jewelry, I might be able to help you," the electrician said to Mother.

"Yes, I have some," she said, quietly. I have no idea how she hid it. Everybody else had handed everything over at the police station in Svencionys.

"Give it to me. I'll show it to the commandant," the electrician said.

Carefully, so that no one else could see what was going on, Mother handed him a pair of diamond earrings, a ring, and a woman's watch with little diamonds.

A little while later, the electrician returned to Mother.

"You're lucky. The commandant loved your jewelry, especially the watch. I think he wants it for his wife," he said, in a hush.

"When are you going to leave?" Mother asked the electrician.

"Oh, the commandant is my friend. He will let me go any time I want," he answered.

Later we heard that the commandant did not let the electrician go and that he was killed with everybody else.

Even though Mother and the electrician had spoken secretively, a husband and wife had overheard them and asked Mother to let them and their two children join us. Mother agreed. Since the payment was only for one family, we came up with a plan. The woman had gray hair and was older than Mother, so we would say she was Mother's mother, and her husband was Mother's husband, our father. Their two children would be Mother's children, our sister and brother.

A few days later, we were called to the police station at the edge of the camp. It was in the evening, and they kept us there for hours. They asked everybody many questions, together and individually. We were scared and very tense. We felt so powerless. After all, they could have kept Mother's jewelry without letting us go.

The other family's youngest, the boy, was about six or seven years old. The police asked him who his mother was. They knew that children usually tell the truth, so they asked the youngest one. But this boy had been told what to say and knew that his life depended on saying the right thing. Children during the war had to be very wise. He pointed to Mother. That saved us all. If the boy had made a mistake, we would have been shot. Finally, they let us go.

We started walking away from that horrible place, not knowing where to go. Not far down the road, we saw a group of farmers carrying shovels walking in the direction of the camp. Mother told me to ask them where they were going. They said they were told to come with shovels and dig graves, for the Jews were to be killed. We'd been in Poligon for two weeks and made it out just before everyone was annihilated.

Since we didn't know where else to go, we went back to Svencionys.

Most of the Jewish community from Svencionys was in Poligon, but a small ghetto for so-called "Nützliche Juden" – useful Jews – had remained. These were shoemakers, tailors, and other skilled laborers,

Alice Singer-Genis with Emunah Herzog

who worked for the Germans. We arrived in the ghetto late at night and slept over at somebody's house.

In the morning, Mother's cousin's maid, Emilka, came to the ghetto. Chaya-Sorel, the one who had escaped from the square before we were marched to Poligon, had sent her. Chaya-Sorel and her husband had no children and treated Emilka like a daughter.

"You must get out of the ghetto quickly. You'll get killed here," Emilka said.

There was no time. She was concerned that people would recognize Mother and Edith as Jews, so she led them out of the ghetto through the back where they wouldn't be noticed. She thought that I, with my blond hair, wouldn't attract attention, so she told me just to cross the street and I would be out of the ghetto, and from there to walk to a small road on the outskirts of town.

It was farmers' market day, in the late afternoon, when the market was finished. A farmer named Mishkello was waiting for us on a quiet little street with his horse and buggy. He was a Lithuanian who used to sell his products to Mother's cousin before the war. They had a good relationship. He took us to his farm. Mishkello knew from Emilka that Father was in Gleboki and that we wanted to join him there. When we came to the farm, they hid us in the barn with the cows and horses. We stayed in the hay at the top of the barn. At night the daughters or the son brought us food. I had been hungry for weeks. So the home-cooked, warm food tasted heavenly to me.

The farmer's wife was very afraid to keep us. They didn't tell the small children that we were hiding on the farm, because they were scared of the neighbors finding out about us. One of the daughters was friendly and smiled when she brought us food, but the other daughter was unfriendly and it was obvious that she didn't like us being there. Mishkello's son, Joseph, wouldn't only come to bring us food, but frequently just visited and sat and talked with us for hours.

After a few days, Mishkello walked to Gleboki to tell Father that we were hiding on his farm and that we wanted to go to Gleboki. Father had heard that Poligon was destroyed and everybody was dead so, of course, he was mourning the loss of his wife and his daughters. When he was told we were alive, he fainted. He asked Mishkello to please bring us to him. Mishkello walked back to Lithuania. It was quite a distance that this good man walked.

I Won't Die Hungry

One night they let us in the house. The farmer's wife heated water in a big kettle and we took a bath. Mishkello had told us that she was scared to death all the time and couldn't sleep at night. She did it out of the goodness of her heart and I'll always remember it. We stayed two weeks on the farm. In the meantime, Mishkello and Joseph made a plan how to get us to Gleboki. I've often thought of that time – the two weeks in hiding after the two weeks in Poligon – as a chapter in my life showing the best and the worst in people.

We left when it got dark. Mishkello and Joseph walked with us. We walked quietly, but when we approached a village, the dogs would bark. It was a giveaway. We tried to stay away from the dogs as much as possible. I can still hear the sound of the barking in the dark, quiet night and remember how scared I was. But we walked fast and covered a lot of territory.

It was morning when we came to a bridge that was between Belarus and Lithuania. I walked with Joseph, and Mishkello walked with Mother and Edith. Mishkello told us that this bridge was guarded, but there was a way to go around the bridge. It took another six kilometers. I was very tired and decided to go across the bridge. Joseph went with me. Mother and Edith took the long way with Mishkello. Luck was on our side. The guards were not there. Nobody was on the bridge. We were in Belarus.

When we came to a town called Postavy, it was getting dark. Mishkello knocked at some people's door – I think he knew them – and asked to let us sleep over. He told them that he was driving a Polish lady and her two daughters to join her husband who worked for the Germans. As I remember, there was a woman, a Belarusian peasant, who let us sleep on the top of the oven. Mother slept closest to the fire, I on the other end, and Edith in the middle. The oven was so hot that Mother's behind got burned, which might seem funny today, but wasn't fun to her at the time. Early in the morning we left. Somehow Mishkello got a horse and buggy and he drove us to Gleboki.

After the terrifying night in prison; the horrendous march from Svencionys to Poligon; the unspeakable two weeks in the camp; the nerve-racking escape just before the camp was annihilated; the two weeks hiding in Mishkello's barn; and the difficult journey across the boarder to Belarus; much of that time Father believing us dead – we were finally together again.

Chapter Four

Unfortunately, we didn't have time to celebrate the reunion for long, because we arrived in Gleboki just as the local government began sending people to the ghetto. The area designated as the ghetto was the poorest section of town called Kisileika. They had built a high wooden fence around it with only one gate which was guarded by the police and their dogs.

We moved to a tiny house, which consisted of two small rooms, a little kitchen, and an outhouse. It had to accommodate the four of us, three aunts (Ella, Celia, and Chaya), and two cousins (Aryeh, Aunt Chaya's son, and little Asya, Aunt Ella's daughter.) Father had hired a Polish truck driver to get Aunt Chaya and Aryeh out from Vilno and bring them to Gleboki.

By this time, Uncle Hirshl, Father's youngest brother who was Aunt Chaya's husband and Aryeh's father, had been taken by the Lithuanian police, the so-called "Hapunes" who took thousands of young Jewish men right away in 1941. The Hapunes said they needed these young men for work but, in reality, most of them were sent to concentration camps or shot right away. We had no idea of his whereabouts. In Vilno the ghetto was downtown, in the same area where the ghetto was in the middle ages, with narrow little streets, very different from the area where we had our house.

On the outskirts of Vilno was an area known as Ponary, where the infamous Ponary massacre took place. It was the mass-murder of around 100,000 people by the German SS and the Lithuanian police. The victims were brought to the edge of pits – which they often had to dig themselves – and shot to death by machine gun fire. It is estimated that some 70,000 Jews were murdered there, along with 20,000 Poles and 8,000 Russians. I don't think that Lipa and his family ever went to the ghetto, but that they were sent to Ponary to die right away. We had lost all contact with them.

Aunt Hannah and Uncle Moshe were extremely worried about their sons who we hoped had fled from Lvov when the Germans took over. It was very difficult for us not to know what had happened to our family members.

Another family, refugees from Vilno, the Feigls – a mother and father and a married son with his wife – lived with us in the house in Gleboki Ghetto. So in total thirteen people lived in this two-room-house. Our room was nothing but beds, maybe a table. The Feigls slept in the other room; two couples in two beds. Somebody slept in the kitchen, but I don't remember who. What I do remember is how well we all got along, in spite of the crowded place, no food, and the fear we lived with. So even though life in the ghetto was harsh and dangerous, it was quiet and peaceful at home. In the evening Aunt Chaya read stories to us by Sholem Aleichem about an orphan – Motl Pesi Tem Chasens – who used to say, "I am lucky to be an orphan." It was sad and funny at the same time, the typical humor of Sholem Aleichem, Jewish humor. We laughed while listening to this and other stories. The younger of the Feigl men had a pretty voice. He sang beautiful Hebrew songs. He sang "Yam Kinneret Sheli" meaning "Lake Tiberius is mine." While his body was stuck in the ghetto, his spirit dreamed about the land of Israel. Throughout my life, when I heard this song, I thought of him. I doubt he ever found out that Palestine became the land of Israel, because as far as we know, all of the Feigls perished when Gleboki Ghetto was annihilated.

When we got there, a "Judenrat," a Jewish government, and a Jewish police force were organized. Everybody worked hard. We thought that work was the answer to survival. As long as the Germans needed our workers, we would stay alive. It was only wishful thinking! But it kept things going for a while.

I worked at the "Marmeladen-Fabrik", the jam factory. It was organized by a Jewish businessman who used to sell chocolate. He came up with the idea of making jam from beets. It didn't cost much to produce and was pretty tasty. He employed young school girls my age – I was fifteen now. His niece was a friend of mine who asked me if I wanted to work there. Our job was to grind cooked beets on a big grinder. A few men worked on a huge machine and cooked the jam according to the director's recipe. The jam factory belonged to the Verpflegungsamt, the office in charge of the food supply for the German Army. Fortunately, as long as we produced well, there were no Belarusian or German supervisors in the jam factory. I heard many stories by others who were beaten up at work. In the Verpflegungsamt was a "Sudentendeutscher" (a German from the annexed Sudetenland) who used yell, "Die Menschheit ist verrückt!" (Humanity has gone mad!) while beating the Jewish slave workers.

Father worked in an oil factory which was also supervised by a Jewish man, the former owner of the oil factory. In the beginning, Mother worked at the hospital in the ghetto and later at a nursery outside the ghetto. It was Father who came up with the idea of the nursery. He suggested to the Judenrat that my Aunt Hannah and Uncle Moshe should run the nursery which they previously owned. This way more people could be employed, Father reasoned. Soon his plan was implemented.

Aunt Hannah and Uncle Moshe received permission to live at the nursery outside the ghetto, in the house that had previously belonged to them, to take care of the big garden. A group of about twenty laborers marched from the ghetto to the nursery every day, among them Mother, Edith, Aunt Ella, and little Asya. Every day fresh fruit, vegetables, and beautiful flowers were delivered to the Gebietskomissar, a high-ranking German official, who was in charge of this and many other important operations in the area. Mother arranged the fresh flowers for the Gebietskomissar.

In the mornings, all Jewish slave workers from the ghetto had to assemble on a square. Sometimes we had to stand in the cold and rain for a long time, waiting to be counted. From there we had to march in columns to our workplaces. We were not allowed to walk on the sidewalks. The sidewalks were for people. We were not considered people; we were Jews. Jews had to walk where the horses walked.

One day, a Belarusian boy who'd been very friendly with Bomka and me before the war walked by me and pretended not to know me. It hurt my feelings deeply. After the liberation, I ran into him again, and he started telling me that Bomka had survived. I just said to him, "You didn't know me then, so I don't know you now," and walked away.

However, I also remember a Polish boy I knew from school but with whom I was never friends. He looked at me and lifted his hat when he passed by our column, which pleased me very much at the time and still does when I think of it.

In the ghetto, food was scarce. We were not allowed to bring in anything. The one and only gate was closely guarded by the Belarusian police. Everywhere, the Germans used the local police and sometimes these policemen were so cruel that they seemed worse than the Germans. Father used to sneak in some oil from the factory, and other family members risked their lives when they smuggled even a few potatoes in. From the Judenrat we got a ration of flour. We peeled the potatoes, cooked them and mashed the peels, and Mother made pancakes.

In the early days of living in the ghetto, Joseph – the farmer Mishkello's son – visited us. He put on a Jewish yellow star and marched in with the workers. What a chance he took to venture into the ghetto; he must have cared for me to do it. I was very touched by this. In 1944, after the liberation, Mother and Father paid Mishkello a visit and were saddened to learn that Joseph had been killed by the Gestapo during the war.

Another day, also in the beginning, a Polish countess, an acquaintance of Aunt Chaya, came to see us in the ghetto. It was very noble of her. She said, "I am surprised how passive you Jews are going to the grave." A short time afterwards, sadly, the countess and her friends were arrested by the Gestapo at a party when they ate and drank and sang Polish patriotic songs. The rumor had it that she was executed by the Gestapo.

As time went on, life in the ghetto became harder and harder. The Germans created a second ghetto for older people. My grandparents were sent there and Uncle Mula, who was not married and lived with them. Since the older people were not considered productive workers, they didn't get food. Father begged the Judenrat to let my grandparents stay with us. "They still can work," he pleaded with the Jewish men in charge. But they didn't want to do it. They said to him in Yiddish, "They will go with 'Kol Hanorim,'" meaning with everybody else.

All over Belarus, Ukraine, and Lithuania, small ghettos were being annihilated. The Jews in these small towns weren't even sent to camps, but were killed right there. Some people escaped the killing and came to Gleboki. We shared our homes and food and found work for them, and our ghetto became even more crowded. They told terrible stories.

Usually the Belarusian or Ukrainian or Lithuanian police or the German soldiers would surround the ghetto and march the people to pits that had been dug before, often by Jews, or by peasants from the surrounding villages. Then the local police or the Germans would shoot the Jews who'd fall into the pits. The bodies were quickly covered with sand. Often Jewish men were forced to carry and bury the corpses of others. There were a few who escaped from the pit, which is what happened to a friend of mine, Slava.

Slava's family left Gleboki and went to the small town of Postavy. They thought conditions were better there. But, not long after they arrived, the entire population of Postavy Ghetto was marched to a pit and murdered. Slava was nine years old at the time. Her parents both died, but she only sustained a minor injury and crawled out from underneath the dead bodies after the shooting stopped. I met her again after the liberation in Gleboki, and we've stayed friends in the States. I have often thought about what it must have been like to have gone through such an experience. Slava is alive today and, until recently, she was a very energetic woman, full of life. Currently she's battling cancer.

In June of 1942, there was a "Sh'chita" in the Gleboki Ghetto. "Sh'chita" is Hebrew and means "Slaughter." We also called it the selection. Everybody was told to assemble on the square in town. Father didn't want us to go. Somehow he knew that our neighbor, who was part of the Jewish police force, had a secret shelter beneath his basement. This man had no qualms about taking his family to the square, as in those days the Jewish policemen were still relatively safe. So he allowed us to descend into his dungeon.

From the cellar, we had to climb down a steep ladder into the blackest possible darkness. The tomb-like structure was tiny, and for two seemingly endless days, the fearful lot of us – Father, Mother, Edith, Aunt Chaya, Aryeh, and I – was huddled together, unable to stretch our legs at the same time. There was no food, but there was a little water which my parents rationed carefully.

When we came out from the shelter, a horrendous devastation awaited us. Immediately, we heard that everybody who lived in the other ghetto had been murdered. Our grandparents and Uncle Mula were dead. There are no words for the grief we felt.

In our ghetto, the people who went to the square were surrounded by

Germans and the Belarusian police. Everybody had to show their work papers. Some were sent to the left and some to the right. Some were sent to live and some were sent to die. It all depended on the jobs we held. The more important jobholders were spared. Who knew what was important and what was not important? I found out that my "Schein" – my work paper – wouldn't have been one of the good ones as soon as I got to the jam factory.

I don't know why Aunt Celia had gone to the square instead of coming with us. Just as a German soldier directed her to step to the side of the people to be killed, she saw the red hair of the chief of the Jewish police out of the corner of her eye. His name was Yudah Blunt. She grabbed his arm and said, "This is my husband." Her voice shook and tears rolled down her face when she told us how close she'd come to being gone.

The people who were sent to be killed were brought to a place called Borok. It was a young forest outside Gleboki. Together with everyone from the other ghetto, they were shot and thrown in pits. Nobody survived. Some men were forced to bury the dead bodies and then were shot also. I understand this was done to my Uncle Mula.

Everybody had lost somebody. Countless families were completely destroyed. In my family, four children had lost their parents and brother. Edith, our cousins, and I had lost our grandparents and uncle. I felt so bad. My grandfather was such a good person, he had helped so many people, and he was killed in such a terrible way. But we didn't have time to grieve our loss. We had to go to work right away.

When I got to the jam factory, it was eerily quiet. Almost all the girls were missing. I took my usual place and started grinding beets, but my girlfriend, who had worked next to me every single day, was not there. I couldn't believe that she was dead, that she'd been killed along with so many others. All day long the empty spot next to me reminded me of what had happened. I was so, so sad. Soon the empty spots in the different workplaces were filled with newcomers. For a long time, even after I was transferred to another work place, I missed her terribly.

I saw Bomka briefly, in 1942, for the first time since we had parted before my family moved to Svencionys. He hardly said a word, and he was very, very upset. His family had been killed already.

I Won't Die Hungry

Even before I saw Bomka, I had heard about the arrest and murder of his father by the Gestapo. Bomka and his family lived in the small town of Plissa where his father now worked in the turpentine factory which he previously owned. One day, the Gestapo chief arrested Bomka's father, accusing him of aiding the partisans. The Gestapo took him to their headquarters in Gleboki and held him there. Bomka rushed to Gleboki in hopes of having his father released. Bomka asked for assistance from the president of the Judenrat and begged them for help, but there was nothing the Judenrat could do. Instead of letting Bomka's father go, the Gestapo tortured and murdered him.

After his father's death, Bomka returned to Plissa with his mother and younger brother. A short time later, the local police invaded the houses of the Jews of Plissa and killed almost the entire Jewish population of this small town right in their homes. When the policemen entered Bomka's house, he hid in the attic. He had called out to his brother, but probably everything happened very fast, and his brother didn't follow him. Powerless, hiding in the attic, Bomka had to hear how just a few steps away these men murdered his mother and his younger brother.

Soon thereafter, Bomka escaped and came to the Gleboki Ghetto, which is when I saw him briefly. It is not surprising that he was extremely sad and didn't talk much. Not until much later did I find out that he survived the Sh'chita in the same Jewish policeman's house as my family did. While we were hovering in the underground shelter, Bomka hid in the attic.

Near the ghetto was a big camp for Soviet prisoners of war. They were treated as badly as the Jews. The Germans were shooting them night and day, and we could hear it in the ghetto. One of the Russian prisoners of war escaped from there and came to our ghetto just after the selection. He joined Bomka and sixteen other boys who escaped and went in search of the partisans.

In the beginning of 1942, small groups of partisans had crossed the frontline from Russia and organized the underground resistance. Bomka was a local boy who knew the people and the language, so when he spoke to the villagers, they readily directed him toward the partisans. The boys wandered in the woods for days until they found a small group of partisans. But joining them wasn't that easy.

"Who are you?" the partisans asked the boys.

"We are Jews. We escaped from the ghetto."
Why do you want to join us?"
"We want to fight the Germans."
"Do you have guns?" the partisans asked.
Of course the boys didn't have guns.
"Go and get armed," the partisans said. "Then you can join us."
"Where can we get arms?" the boys asked.
"Kill some Germans, and bring us theirs."

Of the eighteen boys who left the ghetto, eleven returned to Gleboki, unable to kill with their bare hands. Seven boys remained, Bomka among them. Before long, he wore the coat and carried the gun of a German soldier. Bomka probably looked like a German, with his blue eyes and blond hair. Soon rumors circulated in the ghetto about Bomka as a brave and heroic partisan but, at the time, we really didn't know much about him.

In spite of the danger we lived in, human emotions were not dead. On the contrary, they were stronger than in peaceful time. My friend, who worked next to me in the jam factory, was in love with a boy she went to school with until our lives were interrupted and we were thrown into the ghetto. We became slaves of a tyrannical regime that forbade us to belong to the human race and treated us like sub-humans. But we were human; they couldn't take it away from us. The boy was also in Gleboki Ghetto. However, he fell in love with a girl who had escaped from another ghetto. She was not only pretty, but had a beautiful singing voice. She sang Polish, Russian, and Italian songs. My friend was heartbroken. The tragedy was that both girls were killed in the selection in Borok.

In the spring and summer, boys and girls met outdoors next to the wall of the ghetto. Jokingly, we called it "Alea Milloshtchy", the Boulevard of Love. We were so very young – teenagers. I personally never ventured there, but I knew about it from my friend. Later, Edith told me that she went there for a walk with a boy she had a crush on.

Not long after the slaughter, all girls at the jam factory were told to stop work and make a line. A short, fat, yelling German army sergeant with a shrill voice came to pick a girl to work in the kitchen. I remember him as if I saw him today. He looked us over and picked me for the job. The girls were in awe, because there was food in the kitchen and we were hungry. They congratulated me as if I had won an award.

The next day I went to the kitchen for the German officers. It turned out that the Jewish woman who was the cook had become sick and was unable to work. I didn't know how to cook, but for the first few days I managed somehow. But then they wanted me to cook pea soup. I didn't know that it had to be stirred. Needless to say, the soup burned and the smell was all over. I was terrified. I was sure they would shoot me. When I went home and told my family, they too were afraid for my life. The next day I returned to work with my heart pounding in my chest and my whole body weak from fear. Luckily the woman who worked before in the kitchen came back that day. So with God's help, they didn't shoot me but sent me to work in the warehouse instead. It was a miracle. One of the many miracles that happened to me. But for the rest of my life, I never, ever cooked pea soup. My husband loved pea soup and had to order it in the restaurant, because he didn't get it at home.

I began to work in a big warehouse for food for the Wehrmacht, the German Army. In the corner was a small room, the office. A tall, blond Jewish girl worked there as a bookkeeper. My job was to write down the "Leergut" – empty bottles, boxes, and that kind of thing. It was easy and I wanted to help the bookkeeper with her job, but she didn't show me anything. She didn't want me to do bookkeeping.

The good part was that the soldier in charge asked us to make liverwurst sandwiches for him and other soldiers. This was my job. We used to hide some sandwiches, and before they got theirs, we ate ours. The bad part was that they went out and locked us in. In case of bombing or a fire, we wouldn't be able to escape. It was frightening to be locked in the big warehouse, which was next to the railroad station. As strange as it may seem, we were glad when the soldiers returned.

More and more often, rumors circulated about the annihilation of the ghetto. When my parents heard these rumors, they sent us out to some Christians they knew who were willing to hide us for a day or two. So Edith and Cousin Aryeh were sent to a former railroad employee and his wife, who lived close to the nursery. They were good, courageous people who dared to shelter these two children. I went to other people to hide, somewhere in Gleboki, not too far from the railroad station where I worked, but for some reason, I don't remember much about it. When it was quiet again, we'd return to the ghetto.

Once there was a big panic in the ghetto, and a lot of people went out to sleep somewhere else. A former neighbor of Aunt Hannah's, a Baptist woman put us up in her barn. Somehow the police knew about people having left the ghetto and searched the whole area. Many people were found and shot immediately. Mother and Aunt Chaya looked through a crack in the barn wall and saw two policemen walk by. We were hiding in the hay.

One policeman said to the other, "Let's go into the barn."

The other one replied, "Michnika is a nice woman. She is not hiding Jews. Let's go."

And they left. Once again, we were one step from death and were saved.

But when I came to work the next day, I was sent to a different warehouse, a flour warehouse. The Jewish girl who did the bookkeeping there was shot the night before. She was hiding just like we were, but she was one of the people who got caught. Now I had to do the bookkeeping. The military man in charge of the flour warehouse was an older man from Bavaria, and he treated me well. He told me to ask God to survive, and not to go to the partisans. I think his cohort didn't tell him that my predecessor was shot. At that time, I thought he knew. He said she was a pleasant girl and a good worker. It was one of the few times since the beginning of the occupation that I was treated like a human being.

There were rumors about Stalingrad. In Verpflegungsamt, where I worked, the younger soldiers were sent to the front and replaced by older men. One officer who'd returned from Stalingrad used to come to the warehouse. He was shot in a leg and was limping. He screamed and cursed all the time and shot his gun wildly. I was terrified of him. Even my boss, the Bavarian soldier, was afraid of him. Another memory that stands out from that time is seeing Russian prisoners of war in Verpflegungsamt and one of them saying to me, "It hurts to see a pretty, young girl like you wearing a yellow star." It was during that time that I became a Zionist. I remember distinctly coming to the conclusion for myself that the only solution for the "Jewish problem" was a Jewish country and a Jewish state.

More and more often we heard the word "annihilation" in the ghetto and we were afraid that the last time was a rehearsal for the worst to come. Father worked feverishly on a plan for how to escape. He was gathering information about where to go and talked it over with Mother. Edith and I didn't know details, but we knew that sooner or later the ghetto would be destroyed and we'd be killed, and that escape was the only way out.

Chapter Five

WE LEFT THE GHETTO IN Gleboki in March, 1943. The morning of the day we fled, Father told me to go to the nursery after I finished work.

We were not allowed to walk alone outside of the ghetto, only to march to and from work in groups. So in order to get to the nursery by myself, I had to take off the Jewish star and walk through the whole town. It was very dangerous and I was extremely frightened. By now I had seen so many horrible things. I knew to be scared of the worst. I tried not to think about what would happen if I was caught. I just kept walking as quickly as I could. But no matter how fast I hurried across town, it felt like it took forever. Fortunately, I was lucky; nobody saw me.

When I arrived at the nursery, Mother, Edith, and the rest of the family who worked in the garden were all there. Only Father, who was employed in the oil factory in another area of town, was still missing. Word had gotten out that my family was preparing to escape, and the other people who worked in the nursery had decided to come with us. We all waited for Father, with great trepidation. How would he get across town by himself? What if something had happened to him? We waited for him for a long time and got more and more worried. It was almost dark when he finally arrived. We were so relieved to see him.

Up until then, I didn't know exactly what Father's plans were. Now he said to us, "We are going to the village of Nevery. Partisans are there. They will help us."

As soon as it got dark, we left town and entered the woods. We were twenty-three people altogether, including the children. It was cold and there was still snow on the ground. We could only walk at night when nobody would see us, and we walked only in the forests and avoided the villages. It took us three long, dark, exhausting nights to get to Nevery. Somehow I don't remember much about how we spent the daylight hours; all I know is that we were cold all the time.

Before reaching Nevery, we had to cross a river. As we approached the river bank, we saw a small boat there. It was only big enough for two to three people, so it took a while until everyone reached the other side. For some reason, the boat tipped when Uncle Moshe and Aunt Hannah made their way across. They could not swim and almost drowned. Uncle Moshe yelled out the prayer "Shema Israel" as he was fighting not to be swallowed by the icy river. Father, who fortunately could swim, jumped in and pulled them out of the water and saved their lives.

When we finally arrived at Nevery, we asked for the partisans. The peasants directed us to a house where some partisans were drinking. As we approached, the partisans came outside, staggering and drunk, and obviously displeased at the sight of us. They pulled out their guns and made us take our boots off and hand them over, together with anything else of value we possessed. Then they put us against the wall of the house, pointed their guns at us, and made us feel like our last moment alive had arrived. But then, for some reason, they changed their mind.

"Get lost, before anyone sees you," one of the men said. Quickly and quietly, they told us about the "Pushcha" – a huge forest, about twenty-five kilometers from Nevery. "There are Jews hiding in that forest," they said and went back inside with our valuable belongings. This was our first meeting with the partisans. Later we learned how lucky we were that they didn't kill us. They weren't supposed to steal from people like us, and in order not to be found out and punished by their superiors, some of the partisans shot the people they stole from.

Meanwhile, unable to return to the ghetto, we headed out again, barefoot in the snow, towards our new destination. I'm not sure people today can even imagine what it's like to walk in the snow with naked feet, especially after having traveled on foot for three long nights already. Mother still had her boots and she gave them to me. Father soon organized material to wrap around everybody's feet. In Belarusian it was called "Parchanki" and commonly used by the peasants who couldn't afford proper footwear.

The Pushcha was a thick, dark forest, a real wilderness. When we finally arrived there, we found an area with several manmade bunkers. Jews who had come from the small town of Miadziol lived inside. We were told that the partisans had attacked Miadziol and that, during the fighting, many Jews from the ghetto there had escaped and come to this forest.

When we arrived at the first bunker, we weren't allowed in. We had been full of hope that now that we had found other Jews, we would be given shelter. We were so exhausted and desperate, and still frightened, of course. But they didn't let us in. They wore rags and looked terrible, the color of their faces an indescribable grayish white, as if they were dead already. To me, they didn't look like human beings. I actually found them scary to look at. We went to the next bunker. The same thing happened again. Ghastly skeletons with hollow eyes covered in gray skin and wrapped in tattered rags staggered outside and told us to go away.

Many, many years later, at a Hadassah convention in Chicago, a very pretty woman approached my sister and me. This beautiful woman had been one of those wretched people, a little girl then, and remembered us. "You looked so well dressed, and not hungry at all," she told us. Neither Edith nor I would have recognized her; to us these ghostlike people all looked the same, and she was just a small child. It goes to show you how relative everything is. Even though we were well familiar with hunger from life in the camp, in hiding, and in the ghetto, had been on an exhausting and seemingly endless trek through the cold, and had gotten robbed and almost killed by the partisans, compared to the people we found in the Pushcha, we were in good shape. But at the time, we certainly felt at the end of our rope and were horrified that fellow Jews wouldn't share their shelter with us.

Not until we arrived at the very last bunker – it was the fourth or the fifth – did someone let us come inside. A young couple with a little boy, about five or six years old, lived there. The bunker was wet; water kept accumulating on the ground in one big, cold puddle. Every single day we worked together for hours to remove the water from the bunker.

I remember the young woman screaming at her son all the time. Her husband was calm, but she seemed crazy to me. I thought it was strange how she could treat her child this way and I felt bad for the little guy. In the ghetto, I had seen parents sacrifice themselves for their children. One of the members of the Judenrat, together with his wife, had stood in the way of the police and let themselves be shot, so their son could escape. I knew other cases where parents gave up their lives for their children. I kept thinking of that when I heard her screaming at the little boy.

During this time, we were always hungry. One day I even fainted from hunger. I remember an old Jewish man with a bushy beard gave me a slice of bread and I opened my eyes. Mother and I soon learned from the others in the Pushcha to go to the neighboring villages and beg for food. We'd knock on doors, always at night, and sometimes people would throw us pieces of bread or potatoes. Sometimes they didn't. I felt they were scared of us. Begging was a new experience for me, something I would never have imagined anyone in my family would ever do. I was surprised at myself that I could do it. It shows that, if one has to, a person is capable of anything. Once I overcame the initial embarrassment, it was easy to beg for food.

Aunt Hannah, Father's sister, even though she was a strong, smart business woman, went through additional hardship in the Pushcha. She just sat on the planks in the bunker, as if paralyzed. Both Uncle Moshe and Aunt Hannah feared for their two boys and desperately hoped they were still alive. But Aunt Hannah couldn't accept the situation, couldn't cope, and was unable to go begging with us. Sometimes strong people cannot cope when weaker people can. It's not so much strength as it is the ability to adapt oneself to the situation. Flexibility was very important.

Fortunately, soon enough it began to get warm outside. Spring had finally come to the Pushcha. Everything was in bloom and life seemed to become a little bit easier.

But one day, early in the morning, when I was outside in the woods trying to clean myself and air out my clothes, I heard a terrible noise. At first, I didn't know where it was coming from, but then I realized it was the sound of heavy guns being fired. I quickly threw my clothes on and ran back to the bunker as fast as I could. It was empty! Everybody had left! I was so scared. I started running in the direction where some of the other people were headed and soon caught up with my family.

The shooting became louder and louder and seemed to be coming closer and closer. Like crashing thunder that doesn't stop. It was absolutely terrifying. We kept running deeper into the woods. The panic we experienced is indescribable. Some of my family, including Edith, had contracted typhoid fever from the other people in the Pushcha. Father had to carry Edith, because she was so weak. We didn't know where we were running. We just followed one another, running all day long, deeper and deeper into the woods. The shooting didn't stop, even came from above, hour after hour, and we kept running, running, running, without any direction, from dawn until dark. At some point, while we ran to escape the shooting, the other people who had left the ghetto with us disappeared. When they left us and where they went, I don't know. All I remember is that, at the end of that day, they were no longer with us. Finally, at night, the shooting stopped, and the Pushcha was dark and quiet like a grave.

Later we found out that this was called a "blockade." It was only the first blockade of several we experienced. The Germans would surround a certain area and then shoot with heavy, loud artillery, sometimes for days. Many people were killed during these attacks. The Germans didn't dare to go into the forest, so this was how they fought the partisans and tried to kill the Jews that were hiding in the woods.

That night, my family started to plan what to do next. We huddled together, and everybody spoke their mind. This area of the forest was too dangerous to remain in. We had to leave the Pushcha, but we had no idea where to go next. Edith had been the first one who got sick with typhoid fever, but it was clear that Uncle Moshe and Aunt Celia also could no longer walk. And who knew who would come down with this very contagious disease next?

We decided that the only place where we could go would be back to Nevery. Father knew a farmer there named Stepan who worked for the partisans. Maybe Stepan would be able to help us find a place to hide. We had to separate temporarily. Mother and Aunt Hannah stayed behind to take care of Edith, Uncle Moshe, and Aunt Celia. Father, Aunt Ella, her little daughter Asya, and I were to go to Nevery.

While in the Pushcha, we met four boys who had escaped together from a place called Lublana. We called them "the Lublaners." Two of the Lublaners came with us on our journey towards Nevery, and two stayed behind with the rest of our family. There we were, walking again, and again only at night. At least there was no snow on the ground now.

I recently spoke with Asya. She lives in Israel now. I told her I was writing down our story and asked her if she remembered the time in the Pushcha; she seemed so little to me then. "I remember," she said. "I was six years old, and I remember it very well."

Chapter Six

Golducha was an area in a large swamp forest, almost impossible to get to unless one knew the terrain well. This is where we eventually built a bunker – a "Zemlanka" – for the winter. But how did we get to Golducha? Actually, I was the one who got us to go there.

This time, when we got to Nevery, we went directly to the farmer Stepan. Nevery was a village that consisted of many farms which surrounded the center of the village. Stepan, who lived at the edge of the forest, worked for the partisans and was a highly influential and well-respected man. We didn't go to seek his help in vain. He told Father that he would find a place for us. In the meantime, we were welcome to stay in a little shed in the woods, where he stored hay. Since it was summer, we were happy to stay in the open storage shed, which really wasn't more than a roof on wooden poles. Stepan was a smart and generous man. We were not the first family that he, his wife, and their children had helped.

Unfortunately, but not surprisingly, Father came down with typhoid fever soon after we got there. After all, he had carried Edith all day during the blockade. He became unconscious, and suddenly the responsibility for everything seemed to rest on my shoulders. At sixteen, I had to function as the head of the family, find food, and figure out where our whole family would move next.

While we were staying in the hay shed, I worked for Doroty, Stepan's wife. Doroty was a tall, good-looking woman. For bread and potatoes, I scrubbed her wooden floor and did different chores. I also walked into the village to try to get some food for Aunt Ella and little Asya. Father was burning up with fever and hardly ate anything. Aunt Ella tried to get him to drink water at least, as did I, when I was with them in the hut.

People in the village called me the girl in the red dress, after the dress I wore when I left the ghetto and remained in throughout our travels. The villagers were kind and took a liking to me. The farmers gave me food in exchange for chores. I was so young and found that people were good to me. I was very lucky for this.

Stepan told me that a young peasant named Andrei would be able to build a shed for us in the middle of a big swamp, in Golducha. I decided to go there with Andrei to see it. Andrei lived with his two sisters in a tiny house on the other side of Nevery, closer to the forest where the dangerous swamps were located. They were very poor, very simple people. They had no parents and lived alone in a house with only one room and one bed.

Andrei came to pick me up and we entered the swampy woods. Few people went there, for fear of drowning in the deadly morass. To get to Golducha, we had to jump from one place to another, careful not to fall in and get swallowed up by the sticky, black earth. But this area of the forest was thought to be safe from the Germans, because it was so treacherous to get there. Even though it was scary in its own way, I knew this was as good a place for my family as I could find. We had nowhere else to go.

Andrei quickly went to work on a hut for us, similar to the hay shed we'd been living in at Stepan's – a roof on several wooden poles, open on the sides. But it took him a few weeks. He built it between the trees, so it blended in and couldn't be detected. As soon as he completed constructing our shelter, we got ready to move Father, Aunt Ella, and little Asya to Golducha. The two Lublaner boys, who had traveled to Nevery with us, would go back to get the rest of my family who had been waiting for us in the Pushcha. I thought I had planned everything well, but it wasn't going to be simple after all.

I remember arriving at Andrei's house the evening we were supposed to move. He wasn't home. Soon I realized that he was out in the village, drinking. He had forgotten all about me. I waited for hours. It was a warm summer night that is as clear in my mind as if it was yesterday. The Lublaners were with me, anxious to leave. They tried to convince me not to wait any longer.

"He's not going to come," they said.

I told them we couldn't go without Andrei, we needed his help to transport my sick father. I was not going to leave my father behind. And how would we find our way safely through the swamp? So I insisted on waiting for Andrei.

"He's not going to come," the Lublaners kept saying, over and over again. They even got angry with me.

After a while, I didn't answer them anymore, didn't even look at them. Even though I was upset with them that they tried to persuade me not to wait, I give them credit that they didn't just leave me alone.

Finally, finally, after hours of waiting, Andrei arrived. He was very drunk and visibly surprised at the sight of us. The Lublaners left immediately, so that they would have enough nighttime hours to walk without being seen. I reminded Andrei about our plans. But you can't have a normal conversation with someone so drunk. I had to talk very carefully to him. He staggered over to their little barn and started putting his horse and buggy together. His horse was a small, pitiful thing, the most wretched horse you ever saw. He was the poorest man in the village and his horse was the shabbiest. Eventually, Andrei got it all together and we were on our way to Stepan's hut where my sick father, Aunt Ella, and Cousin Asya were waiting.

When we came to pick up my family in Stepan's hut, Andrei took one look at Father and said, "The man is dead. I'm not going to take a dead man." Andrei was still drunk and there seemed to be no way to persuade him. "I'm not taking a dead man," he repeated, slurring his words.

As if things weren't difficult enough, a Jewish boy named Simcha who lived with his family in a close-by "Zemlanka" – a bunker – came over and tried to talk me out of going to Golducha.

"The Germans are going to attack there," Simcha warned me. I had a feeling that he had a crush on me and did not want me to leave for selfish reasons. But Aunt Ella believed him and started to cry, afraid of a German attack in Golducha.

There I was, after all my troubles – sixteen years old and fighting everyone. I had to make the decision between life and death, not knowing for sure what the right thing to do was. I decided that we would go to Golducha. The Lublaners would bring the rest of our family soon, and we had to go somewhere.

I don't know how I finally talked the drunken Andrei into taking

Father, who couldn't even walk. But eventually, Andrei and I carried him out and Andrei put him on the wagon and we all left. Most of the way, Aunt Ella, Asya, and I walked, because the horse was so weak and slow. I think we walked faster than that pitiful creature.

It was still dark when we arrived at Andrei's house. He and his sisters left their one and only bed to Father. My aunt, cousin, and I stayed in their barn. This is something I will remember for the rest of my life. The reality that poor people can be so giving, without even realizing how good they are, sustained me through all hardships.

Father started feeling a little better after being able to rest in a bed. On top of the typhoid, he had developed pneumonia and was coughing hard. There were no antibiotics in those days, no medicines at all where we were, but I found somebody from the village who put "Bankes" on Father's chest. It was an old-fashioned treatment of placing heated glass on the body to increase circulation, and he started to improve.

A few days later, Mother, Edith, Aunt Celia, Aunt Hannah, Uncle Moshe, and a few other people arrived from the Pushcha with the Lublaners. As soon as they came into Andrei's small house, I told them they must all go to our hut in Golducha. But they didn't want to go. After all the time they had spent in the forest, they simply didn't want to leave the shelter of a real house, no matter how small it was.

"You can't stay here," I said to them. "It's too dangerous. You must go to the hut Andrei built for us."

They didn't want to leave.

Here I was, having to fight again. I had to push them out the door.

"Please, go with Andrei to our hut," I pleaded.

Finally they agreed and Andrei took them to Golducha. Aunt Ella and little Asya went with them too. Only Mother and I remained with Father. He was so happy to see her that he said, "Now I will be all right."

Just as soon as the others had left, Stefka, Andrei's sister, burst into the house.

"Run away! Germans are in the village center!" she said, her voice filled with terror.

We grabbed Father under his arms and hurried out of the house into the forest. All day long we heard the heavy shooting. We wandered around in the swamps and really had no idea where we were. It was the same thing all over again as in the Pushcha, except Father was very weak and there was the additional danger of drowning in the mud. When it was getting dark, I heard somebody calling my name.

"Asya! Asya!" It was a man's voice, and it echoed through the woods. I can still hear it in my mind. "Asya! Asya!"

"Don't answer," Mother said. She was afraid it was one of the Germans. So at first I didn't answer. But the shouting didn't stop, and seemed to come closer.

"Asya! Asya!"

Finally, I took heart and answered.

It was Andrei! Andrei was looking for me! If I hadn't answered, we would probably have died there in the woods and swamp. Instead, Andrei led us to our hut, where the rest of our family was anxiously waiting for us. Once again we were all together.

Later we found out that all of Nevery, which was considered a partisan village, was burned down to the ground. However, by the time the Germans attacked, not a single partisan was around. They had left before the Germans attacked. This was the strength of the partisans: they fooled the Germans time and time again. Unfortunately, the local population as well as people like us suffered the consequences. Andrei, Stefka, and their older sister – I'm sorry I forgot her name – lost their home and went to another village to live with family. We lost contact with them, but I am still filled with tremendous gratitude when I think of these generous and kind people who risked their lives to help us. Without them, I would not be writing these words.

We moved into the hut. Edith, Uncle Moshe, and Aunt Celia had recovered, and Father was feeling better. But now Aunt Hannah – who had cared for Uncle Moshe – and I got sick with typhoid fever. Mother took care of us. We had no medicine, not even a blanket. I was lying on the bare ground, unconscious and delirious, because of my high fever. I couldn't eat. I only drank some water that Mother boiled on the campfire. Somehow I survived, as did the rest of the family, without medication. We were lying on the ground and Mother Earth was our bed. I remember hallucinating and singing. Aunt Hannah and I were the last of our family to have typhoid fever.

It's interesting that Mother never got it. She wasn't a strong woman.

Before the war she was often sick. She had problems with her gallbladder and used to go to spas to drink waters that were supposed to help her. During the war, however, she had no health problems. Maybe it was due to the simple food. And I think she got some kind of vaccination when she worked for the health department in Svencionys. Perhaps that's why she didn't contract typhoid fever even though she took care of us and lived through the same conditions as we did.

Just as I began to feel better, the Germans attacked again. The thundering artillery fire seemed to come from everywhere, especially from above. Once again, everybody ran wherever they could in an incredible panic. Mother, Edith, and I ran away together. I remember grabbing a loaf of bread as we fled from the hut. We ran deep into the thick woods. It was very wild there, the trees grew close together, and we hid in the groves between the trees. Huddled together with my family, I started eating the bread I had brought from the hut and offered some to them.

"How can you eat when they're shooting at us like this?" Mother asked.

"If I am shot, at least I won't be hungry when I die," I answered and meant it.

This went on for a few gruesome days. Finally, one night, the deafening noise stopped and quiet descended over us again. Somehow, we went back and found our hut. Everybody eventually returned – it was a miracle no one got killed by the relentless shooting or drowned in the swamps – and our everyday existence continued again.

In retrospect, I've come to believe there were informers among the peasants around Golducha, as well as in Nevery and near the Pushcha. Perhaps it was even the villagers whom we begged for food. How else would the Germans have known to burn down the houses in Nevery, to shoot at us hiding in the Pushcha, and then again in Golducha?

During the spring and summer of 1943, we were surrounded three times, blockaded and shot at with heavy artillery. But we were grateful that we could run into the forest to hide. People in the ghetto had nowhere to run to when they were surrounded by the police. They were taken to their graves, thrown into the pit and killed. We heard, before the end of that summer, that the entire ghetto in Gleboki was annihilated.

All the people who had remained there were murdered and the ghetto ceased to exist.

Yet our life went on. Aunt Celia had met a man in the Pushcha. His name was Velvel and he joined our family when we left for Golducha. The two of them became close and wanted to get married. There was no formal dating in the woods; everything moved quickly. So Uncle Moshe performed the marriage ceremony in front of a fire in the woods of Golducha. Father and a man called Yankel were the witnesses.

We knew the summer was coming to an end soon and we wouldn't be able to stay in the open hut much longer. So the men decided to build a bunker – a "Zemlanka" – on a small island in the swamp. The men did most of the work, but the women and children helped too. Luckily, toward the fall, a few more people joined us. Among them was my Aunt Chaya, together with her thirteen-year-old son, Aryeh, and a friend whom she had met among the partisans. Everybody worked together to build this bunker, where we would be better protected from the cold.

And indeed, when winter arrived, it was warm in our Zemlanka, because it was deep in the ground. We slept on wooden planks which the men had built right into the bunker. Sometimes, during the long, dark winter nights, we heard the wolves howl. The nights were so quiet and the air so clear that we couldn't gauge how far they were and we hoped that they weren't coming closer.

We were the first to build our home there, the first house on the island. Later others built bunkers there, too. Our Zemlanka became home to many Jews who escaped from the ghetto as well as partisans who passed through often. There was a young girl named Eadla who had somehow arrived in Golducha. Quiet and withdrawn, Eadla had lost most of her family in Gleboki. We took her in and Father said, "I now have three daughters." Eadla stayed with us until after the liberation.

I remember another little boy, blond with blue eyes, who escaped from a different ghetto and came to us in Golducha. He never spoke a word. We weren't sure if he was born that way. I always felt he stopped speaking after the shock of losing his family. He arrived with a severe leg wound and Mother took care of him. She showed me how to clean the wound and change the bandage. I soon did this for him every day. It gave me deep satisfaction.

Many partisans had acquired a terrible skin rash. Mother invented a medicine, from pork fat and dynamite powder. The dynamite looked like bars of soap and contained sulfa. The partisans put this explosive under the railroad tracks to blow up trains headed toward the front. They also used it to destroy bridges. Mother crushed these bars into a powder, and she boiled the pork fat until it had a creamy consistency. Mixed together, this became a soothing ointment which helped with the pain and the itching.

On the other side of the forest, there was a small village called Krizanowka. It was made up of only three homes. A new group of partisans settled in the big farm house closest to the woods. They called themselves "Boevoi Otriad," which meant "The Fighting Unit." Men and women would come and go in small groups. They had cows and horses and they needed somebody to take care of their animals. So Father tended to the horses, together with Uncle Moshe. Uncle Velvel, Celia's husband, was in charge of the cattle and used to slaughter and cut up the cows. The partisans took the beef, but they didn't want the legs or heads of the cows. This was a big help and saved us from hunger. Father loaded the horse-carriage with the legs, heads, and other parts of the butchered cows and distributed them also among some Jewish people who were hiding several kilometers from us. The women cooked what the partisans rejected and, with some bread and potatoes, it was decent food. This is how we survived the winter.

Aunt Hannah was an excellent cook. She made all kinds of dishes. All the cooking took place outside, on the fire; there was no stove and one couldn't cook in the bunker. I especially remember the dumplings she made from potatoes, filled with meat. They were delicious. She named this dish "Saltinosy." From the bones, she made wonderful broth and soup.

Aunt Hannah was a strong woman who could be very bossy. By now she had overcome the paralysis she experienced after we first left the ghetto. I remember how she saved me once. We'd gone to the village together, and we came across a young peasant. I think he was drunk.

"I want the young girl," the peasant said and pointed to me. But Aunt Hannah carried a stick with her and fought him off.

One of the other people who had joined our family in Golducha was Yankel, the same man who had been a witness at Aunt Celia and Uncle Velvel's wedding. Yankel had flaming red hair and a red beard. He had lost all his family. I don't know how he came to live with us. He was an angry man and didn't listen to anybody, except to Aunt Hannah. He would do whatever she told him.

"Yankel," she'd say. "Make a fire."

And he would make a fire.

"Yankel, we need more wood," her stern voice could be heard saying.

And he would go and collect wood.

Aunt Hannah was the only one who could boss this big, angry man around. He was very handy, no one chopped wood like he did. It was interesting how these relationships formed.

Cousin Aryeh, who had lived with the partisans before he and Aunt Chaya joined us in Golducha, told me many stories about Bomka. Yes, the boy I had gone out with during my first year in Gleboki, the boy that hardly spoke a word when I saw him in the ghetto – he was famous among the partisans for his courage and wits. I was very impressed.

The group Bomka joined was sent from the Soviet Union and was called the "Medvediev Otriad" which later became a brigade. Because Bomka was a local boy who knew the Belarusian language, local customs, the countryside, and the people, he was very useful to them. He also had an excellent sense of direction and could find his way through the woods and across the swamps. So they put him in the reconnaissance, which was an important and dangerous position. He sustained a gunshot wound in the arm, and a nurse from Gleboki, a Jewish girl who had joined the partisans, took care of him. I remembered her.

The job of the partisans was to sabotage the German war effort. They put explosives under the railroad tracks to destroy the trains that carried supplies to the German soldiers on the front. They had to find out when the trains came, where they were going, and to camouflage the explosives so that they could not be detected. They also attacked smaller groups of Germans. The Germans attacked and blockaded us and burned villages like Nevery, but they never went into the woods. They were terrified of the partisans.

When his father was killed, Bomka promised himself to avenge his father's death and kill Kopferberg, the Gestapo chief who arrested, tortured, and executed Bomka's father. So when Bomka joined the partisans, he developed a plan for how to kill Kopferberg.

Alice Singer-Genis with Emunah Herzog

First Bomka decided to scare Kopferberg. Under significant risk, Bomka would sneak into town at night and put posters up, saying that he, Bomka, the son of Genichowicz who was murdered on the order of Kopferberg, was going to kill the powerful commander to avenge the blood of his father. The posters appeared every night in different places: next to the town hall, in the market place, even next to the police station. Bomka also wrote letters to Kopferberg and signed them "Bomka."

At first Kopferberg underestimated the threat. But slowly fear overtook him. In order to catch Bomka, Kopferberg sent out farmers who knew Bomka to look for him in the woods. Kopferberg even asked the president of the Judenrat to convince Bomka that he, Kopferberg, was not involved in the murder of Bomka's father.

Bomka watched Kopferberg carefully. He found out that Kopferberg was going to travel by car to Minsk. Bomka and a few other partisans waited in ambush. Bomka was the leader of the group. For hours they hovered behind trees, in freezing rain. Finally, around 10:00 in the morning, they heard the sound of engines. The Gestapo was traveling in two cars; Kopferberg in the first car, together with another officer and the driver. In the second car were Gestapo guards.

As the cars approached, the partisans opened fire. The other officer was killed right away. Kopferberg was seriously wounded, and his driver, also wounded, drove him to the hospital in Minsk. The Nazis in the other car returned fire. The partisans were outnumbered, yet they left several dead Nazi soldiers on the road and fled into the woods. Kopferberg died in the hospital soon after he got there. Rumor has it that his dying words were, "The Jew has killed me."

It was after this happened that Bomka became famous in the underground among the partisans and the local people.

Another story Aryeh told me many times was this: In order to survive, the partisans had to take food and sometimes clothing from the peasants. Bomka didn't like to do this. He always got along well with the local people, and the peasants were fond of him. Since Bomka was in the reconnaissance, he found out when the farmers were ordered to deliver food – bread, potatoes, meat, eggs, and milk – to the Germans. So the partisans stopped the farmers on the road, surrounded them, and confiscated the food.

The peasants were scared and said to Bomka, "What will we tell the Germans? They're going to kill us when we don't deliver."

Bomka told them not to worry. He wrote a note, telling the Germans that he had confiscated the food for the partisans, and signed it "Bomka." Believe it or not, the Germans honored the note.

Bomka was Cousin Aryeh's idol, and he loved telling me about his hero over and over again. And I loved listening and wondered if Bomka still thought of me and if I would see him again.

One story that Aryeh told me stuck in my mind for a different reason. There was a German spy, a woman, who turned many individuals over to the Gestapo and who created much suffering for the local people. They all hated her. She went to church on Sundays, so one day, a few men walked into the church, grabbed her under her arms, and dragged her to the partisans. After brief deliberations, the Russian partisans told a Jewish guy to shoot her. He was a friend of Bomka's, also from Plissa.

"I cannot shoot a woman who has no arms," he said. And he didn't.

So they got a Russian guy to shoot her, and they made fun of Bomka's friend. But I always had and still have respect for someone like this; I feel it was the Jewishness in him.

Mother healed many people. Once she saved the life of a girl who was sexually active and got venereal disease from a partisan. She was a pretty, young girl who was not married. Her life was in danger. So Mother went to the doctor in the Boevoi Otriad. She presented the case and told him the girl contracted the disease from a partisan in his unit. The doctor, a blondish man who stands out in my memory, gave Mother some medicine to be used as an internal rinse against the infection. She walked three kilometers through the forest to the village where the girl was staying with some farmers. I often accompanied Mother on her six-kilometer hike to treat the young girl with the rinsing medication. Eventually, the girl was cured. It was then that I decided: If I survived, I would become a doctor.

I spent as much time as I could outside. Mother didn't like me to wander off by myself, but I cherished some solitude in the wilderness. I would venture out for hours, find a sunny spot, and dream about Bomka, about going to the university, becoming a doctor, having a family, and whatever any young girl might have dreamed about.

When I think of Golducha, I am grateful to the swamps and forests that sheltered us and saved our lives. Whenever I look at trees I love them. I remember they were our friends. When people betrayed us, they protected us. I will always remember Andrei, Stefka, and their older sister, who took us into their poor home and gave their only bed to my sick father. My parents, too, always helped people who were less fortunate and in need of assistance.

In the spring of 1944, nine months after Aunt Celia's wedding, a little girl was born in our bunker. Mother delivered the baby. She was named Sarah – we called her Sorahle – after Aunt Celia's, Aunt Hannah's, and Father's mother, my grandmother, who'd been killed in the Gleboki Ghetto.

By this time, our area was considered a partisan zone. It was like a country within a country. Finally, we felt free to move around. We began going to the small village where the Boevoi Otriad was stationed more often and spoke with the partisans and got to know them by first names. I admired the brave partisans and, of course, always thought of Bomka. The partisans were people from all walks of life. You could meet a college professor, or a doctor, or a plain thief, or worse. Many of the partisans were escaped prisoners of war.

One of the mistakes Hitler made was the mistreatment of the prisoners of war. They were shot, like the Jews. I remember, near the ghetto in Gleboki, there was a POW camp. We heard the shooting at all hours. In the beginning, the Soviet soldiers surrendered in the thousands, but when they found out that they were going to be shot, they stopped surrendering. Most of the prisoners of war who were able to escape joined the partisans. Some Belarusian and Lithuanian policemen left these collaborating forces and became partisans. Local peasants also joined and, of course, Jewish boys and girls who escaped from the ghetto. The partisan movement became a strong force. Further west of us, there was actually a Jewish unit who had escaped from the Vilno Ghetto, and who fought in Belarus and Lithuania.

The partisans were very secretive and extremely mobile. We never knew where they were going or what exactly their current mission was. Some of the higher ranking partisans had so-called partisan's wives. This meant they were wives only during the war. After the liberation, many stayed together, but many did not. There was a redhead whose "wife" was Nina, a nurse. When she was away on a mission, her husband looked for girls in the village. I remember that the farmer's daughter, Glasha, a plump, pretty blonde, liked to flirt with the partisans. I became friendly with a tall Siberian and his "wife" Jenia who was also a nurse. Both of these couples stayed together, and our paths crossed again after the liberation.

One day, while I was visiting in the house by the forest's edge, a partisan I hadn't seen there before started talking with me. After a brief conversation, he told me he was an escaped policeman from Svencionys. I felt a shiver down my spine but I kept my composure. I had learned during the war not to show my emotions.

Sometimes men who worked with the partisans parachuted from planes and landed in our area. We found the parachutes and used the material for clothing. The material was beautiful, an off-white silk. Most of them were traveling west. Even some Spaniards stopped at the village before continuing westward. These were the children of the original Spaniards who had trained in the anti-fascist movement in Russia.

Once I came into the village and met a parachutist. He was tall and sturdy, his blond hair disheveled. He seemed very old to me, at least thirty. I assume someone told him that I was Jewish, because he approached me and immediately started telling me about himself.

"I'm Jewish," he said, "from Lithuania. I've been in Russia since the beginning of the war. I didn't know there were any Jews here. None of these partisans are Jewish, are they?"

"No," I said, "not one of them."

"So what are you doing here?" he asked.

"I live in a Zemlanka with my family."

His face lit up. "Do you think I could meet them?"

"Sure," I said. "It's only a short walk through the swamp. You want to come with me now?"

Overjoyed, he nodded.

When we walked into our Zemlanka, I heard Aunt Hannah murmuring in Yiddish. "What is that girl thinking to bring a total stranger here? Doesn't she know she's putting us all in danger? Hasn't she learned anything? She brings just anyone here."

But Mother welcomed the man in her customary warm and gracious manner, and eventually Aunt Hannah stopped and handed him a bowl of soup and a slice of bread. He stayed only for a day, and continued westward.

Not much later, a most wonderful surprise happened: Bomka showed up at our Zemlanka in the woods! He said it was very difficult to find us. He kept asking the villagers, but none of them would tell him where we lived, which he acknowledged to be a good thing. We were so happy to see him, especially Cousin Aryeh and I, of course. Bomka couldn't stay very long, but I knew it meant a lot that he went through all the trouble to visit me. I showed him my favorite places in the woods. Soon it was clear that we were still boyfriend and girlfriend, after all this time. Both of us had been through so much since we were first high school sweethearts. It was hard to say goodbye when he left.

In the early summer of 1944, we heard rumors that the Germans were surrounding the woods and forests. And then we started hearing it ourselves. It was different than the blockades in the past, because it was the whole frontline moving. The Russians were going west, the Germans were retreating and, as they were retreating, they were blockading and destroying many areas.

We expected the worst. There was nothing we could do. There was no place to go. The shooting went on day and night. This situation lasted for weeks and weeks. We heard stories of how people in other areas like ours were surrounded and caught alive, and we knew this was coming our way. Every day for weeks we were expecting it, could hear it in the distance; it seemed to be coming closer all the time. How can one even imagine such tension today?

And then, one day, suddenly, the shooting stopped. After seemingly endless weeks, the forest was quiet. Somehow our little area had been left alone. We heard the Russians come in. That's when we decided to return to Gleboki.

We started walking back.

I Won't Die Hungry

Partisans in Ostrovitz, Belarus. Bomka is in the center of the front row holding the map on the viewer's right.
(1944)

Partisans in Ostrovitz, Belarus. Bomka is on the black horse on the viewer's left.
(1944)

Chapter Seven

When we arrived at Uncle Moshe and Aunt Hannah's little house on the outskirts of Gleboki, the nursery was no longer in operation. The house was empty. So we just walked in and stayed. There was a large kitchen, a big dining room, and two bedrooms. My parents, Edith, Eadla – the girl my family had "adopted" – and I stayed in one bedroom and Uncle Moshe, Aunt Hannah, Aunt Ella and her little Asya in the other. Aunt Celia, Uncle Velvel, and Sorahle went back to Svencionys, where Uncle Velvel was from. Aunt Chaya and Cousin Aryeh found a place to live in town. Her husband Sholom was previously drafted into the Soviet Army.

There were nine of us living in very close quarters, yet our small house was open to everyone who needed a roof over their head. People who came from Russia, boys and girls who had no family, were welcome to stay with us until they found a place of their own. Food was still scarce, but we made due. Somehow Uncle Moshe soon had a cow again, and Mother and Edith learned to milk her. I never did.

One day, right in the beginning after we returned to Gleboki, we heard the rumbling noise of military tanks on the road, and became aware of much commotion. All the townspeople spilled out on the street. We also went out and looked at the tanks rolling and roaring through town. I remember it as if it was today, when suddenly we recognized the men on one tank: They were our partisans from the Boevoi Otriad! They immediately recognized us too. They stopped and came off the tank, greeted us by name, and talked with us. Everybody around us was quite impressed. We were very happy to see them after everything we'd been through together. I was especially pleased about seeing my Siberian friend – whose name unfortunately escapes me – and his wife, Jenia. They ended up getting married and settling in Gleboki.

One evening, the mayor of Gleboki brought a Russian general with his wife and children over. His wife was Finish, a courteous, quiet woman. The front was not far from us in Eastern Prussia and Poland. The general wanted his wife and children to stay in Gleboki so that they were close to him. She and the children stayed with us until they found an apartment. She promised us that she would let us know when the war was over right away, since she would be privy to this information through her husband. When the time came, she kept her promise.

It was wonderful to be alive and safe from danger, no longer afraid of being shot. My parents went back to work immediately. Father, as a lumber specialist, got a job as director of a government owned lumber company. Mother went back to work in a hospital. My Siberian friend from the Boevoi Otriad became the head of the finance department and hired me for the summer. All I wanted was to go back to school, but school was closed until the fall.

Every morning, when I walked into the office, the Polish girls made fun of me because I was still wearing the same army boots I wore back in Golducha. A Jewish partisan had given them to me early on in Nevery, and I had worn them ever since.

"You look like a Russian," they said and giggled.

At that time, women didn't wear boots – especially not in the summer! – and Polish women were particularly conscious of their clothing. There is something about Polish women and fashion; it's so important to them. Under Soviet rule, the shoemakers now worked in a government-run workshop. Fortunately, I received a special permit from my boss to get shoes made. We put the order in right away, but my new shoes weren't ready until the end of the summer. It felt like it was taking forever!

We still didn't know what had happened to Cousin Mira and to Uncle Lipa's family. Throughout our ordeals, Mother had always worried about her niece who had stayed in Vilno with Mother when the rest of Mother's family moved to America and to Palestine in the 1920s. Mira had lived with us until she finished nursing school and then joined her parents in Palestine. She was like a daughter to Mother. In 1939, Mira had come back to Vilno to visit us and her fiancé, Sima, a young doctor. Against Father's advice, she did not return to Palestine when the war began. She and Sima were briefly with us in the beginning in Gleboki, but then got married and went to Vilno. We had no idea of their whereabouts.

So one day, soon after we returned to Gleboki from Golducha, Mother decided to go to Vilno and look for Mira. I don't think Mother even told Father about her plan. She got a ride on one of the trucks that went back and forth between Gleboki and Vilno. But she hadn't considered that in Vilno the war was still raging. As she walked through the streets of the city that had once been her home, bombs started falling and panicky people rushed to shelters. Fortunately, a doctor by the name of Libo recognized Mother and approached her.

"Mrs. Singer, what are you doing here?" he asked.

Dr. Libo shook his head when she explained herself and quickly took her with him to a bomb shelter. Mother returned to Gleboki without news. It would still be a while until we found out what had happened to Mira.

But Aunt Hannah and Uncle Moshe soon received devastating news. Their older son, their beautiful Niunka, was dead. Together with his younger brother, Elusha, he had spent quite some time in Siberia working for the railroad. Niunka was in charge of the railroad in a town near Omsk, and Elusha got a job as an inspector at the railroad company's cafeteria. There were two types of restaurants in the Soviet Union: one for the common folk, and one for the party officials and VIPs. Elusha inspected the latter, and thus he didn't suffer hunger in those days and neither did his brother.

In 1943, as the front moved from east to west, Niunka was sent to Kharkov, in the Ukraine. He was part of a team of engineers who repaired the railroad that was destroyed either by German bombs when it was on Russian territory, or before, while it was on German territory, by the partisans. The engineers worked at night. One day, in bright daylight, a single German plane flew over their area dropping bombs. Niunka and a few other officers were playing cards in one of the wagons when the bombs fell and they all were killed. In my opinion, Aunt Hannah and Uncle Moshe never quite recovered from this loss. Meanwhile Elusha had joined the Polish Army and, as far as we knew, was still alive.

Not long after our arrival in Gleboki, a toothache I had while in the woods returned. In hiding, nothing could be done; I just had to live with it and thankfully it subsided. We were told there was a dental clinic in town, a few kilometers from where we lived. I walked to the dental clinic. When it was my turn to see the dentist, he looked at my teeth and, without an x-ray, he told me that he'd have to pull one of my molars. He didn't give me an anesthetic or an injection of Novocain. He just took the pliers and pulled with formidable force. I had never had a tooth pulled. The pain was unbelievable. So while he was pulling, I was yelling. He told me to be quiet because I was scaring the other patients in his office. After he finished the job I started walking back. I stopped at Aunt Chaya's who lived in town. She let me lie down on her bed and I fell asleep from exhaustion. I slept for a few hours, got up, and walked home. But this was nothing compared to what Edith went through.

Edith had an attack of appendicitis, so Mother took her to the hospital. They didn't even give her anesthesia, only a local injection. She felt the terrible, terrible pain. My toothache was severe, but to have one's abdomen cut open and operated on without anesthesia! The doctor was an excellent surgeon, but they did not have anesthesia and had to operate without it in order to save Edith's life.

In the fall the schools reopened and what I had dreamed about so many times finally came true. After three years of interruption by a death camp, life in the ghetto, dangerous journeys, and hiding in the woods, I could go back to school.

All I wanted was to study. I only needed two more years to graduate. The students in my class were all younger than I was; they hadn't lost three years. And I was the only Jewish girl in the whole school. Before the war, more than half of my class was Jewish. At that time, there were two schools in Gleboki, a Russian and a Belarusian one. Edith went to the Russian school which was for the younger students. There were a few Jewish children in her school.

Even though I was extremely happy to resume my schooling, I didn't feel comfortable in the beginning. Some of the students were very unfriendly to me, although others were friendly and kind. The students, for the most part, were from the villages surrounding Gleboki. During the German occupation, the peasants were able to afford to send their children to school. After a while, the other students came to know me. I even participated in a play which was organized by one of our teachers.

The war was still going on. In 1944, when the Soviet army liberated us from the German occupation, many young boys and men were taken

I Won't Die Hungry

to the army. And our Jewish boys, who had survived Hitler, were taken into the army. Some were killed, others crippled for life.

Bomka, the boy I was in love with, had become the military commander of a town called Ostrovitz. His partisan brigade broke through the German line and liberated this town. He was put in charge of Ostrovitz until the Russian Army came in and established a civilian government. I wrote him a letter and suggested that he should come to Gleboki and get a job. I feared that otherwise the Russians would draft him into the army like they did with most partisans. So Bomka also returned to Gleboki. He soon got an important government job.

He lived with us in our small house. He slept on a make-shift bed in the room with Aunt Hannah, Uncle Moshe, Ella, and little Asya. Something quite unusual happened to him. Peasants who knew Bomka and his family returned some of his family's possessions, including a cow, heavy silver from his grandparents, and a silver pocketbook that had belonged to his mother. He didn't even know about these things. It shows how much the local people thought of Bomka. We heard countless stories about Jews who, after surviving the German hell, returned to their homes and nothing was given back to them. Instead, they were chased away and several were even killed.

Bomka brought the cow with him, and the additional daily pail of milk was a big help to us. There were many mouths to feed in our small house. We cooked together and ate together. The food was plain, but we were not hungry anymore.

At the end of our busy days, when everyone else had gone to bed, Bomka and I spent many evenings in the kitchen. The war was still raging close to us in Eastern Prussia and Poland. We were very much aware of it. The only furniture was a large table and simple chairs. One dim light bulb dangled from the ceiling. We didn't care. To us it was as good as it would be today to go on a date to a fine restaurant. The main feature of the kitchen was a large, wood-burning oven. It wasn't fancy, encased simply by white-washed walls, but I still remember the warmth of the wall against my back while talking with the boy I loved. Occasionally, he'd throw a log into the stove and the light of the fire illuminated his handsome face.

Sometimes, I would try to get him to tell me about what it was like for him with the partisans. I admired him for his bravery. At a time when we were helpless as a people, he was strong and took action and I loved him for this. He truly was my hero. But he didn't think of himself as a hero and was reluctant to talk about it even then.

"I did what I had to do," he said.

What always worked was asking him about the horse that was his means of transportation in the reconnaissance. Bomka loved his black horse and could go on and on about its virtues. And I loved looking at his enthusiastic face when he talked about his four-legged friend.

Once I asked him if he wasn't afraid to put his life on the line all the time. The sound of his voice still rings in my ears.

"When I lost my family, I didn't care if I lived or died."

But I know he was very much alive then, and he had a great sense of humor and enjoyed making me laugh. It was during those evenings in our simple kitchen that our romance really blossomed.

Another lovely memory is the day when we went for a sled ride in a horse-drawn, open sled. The snow sparkled in the sunshine and the cold wind blew in our faces, but we were bundled up and very comfortable. Bomka's ease commanding the horse was impressive. And, occasionally, we went to the movies. They were showing mostly war pictures, displaying the bravery of the Russian soldiers.

On May 9, 1945, the war ended.

I went to school as usual. My classmates were crazy with happiness. I was swept away with this mood and was as happy as can be. Our physics teacher – a war invalid and usually a very unhappy man – got drunk and was literally on the floor with euphoria. Before that day, as the only Jewish girl in the class, I had felt like an outsider. That day was completely different. Everybody kissed and hugged me. The joy I felt was overwhelming. I had been hoping for this day for six years of my young life, had waited for it since September of 1939. It was the happiest day of my life.

But it was not a happy day for everyone. I remember Bomka, who had lost his entire family, lying down and crying bitterly. Many thought about our dear ones who hadn't survived to see the end of the war.

Yet I was young, healthy, and I had my family and a wonderful boyfriend who was widely admired and regarded as a hero. I felt that my future looked bright and happy. My dream to become a doctor since the time I helped Mother with the wounded had not changed. I worked hard and completed the last two grades of high school in one year. In the fall of 1945, Mother went with me to Minsk to apply to the Medicinski Institute, the medical school.

By now, the Soviet regime had fully taken over. In order to travel anywhere by train one needed a special permit, called "Comandirovka." Since Father was a director at a government-owned lumber company, he was able to write these permits, and we had no difficulties traveling on that account. But the trains were awful: slow and screeching, overcrowded, with worn-out interiors and hard benches, and passengers who traveled long distances snoring in bunk beds above our heads. Mother and I were among the few civilians on the train, squeezed between scores of Russian soldiers. Even after living in the forest, I remember the train ride from Minsk to Gleboki and back as very uncomfortable. Yet I gladly took any discomfort as long as it would enable me to go to medical school. And indeed, I was accepted.

The next time, Father accompanied me to find a place to live. The town of Minsk had been completely destroyed by the war. The medical school, partially in ruins, was in the center of the city. The streets were dark at night, as there was no electricity in most areas. At least the library was intact. But it was impossible to find housing in the city. Four and five families lived in one apartment.

Somehow Father found a poor family in the outskirts of town willing to let me sleep in their dining room which also functioned as the living room. There was only one other room in the house where they all slept. Father promised them to bring meat and other food in exchange for my bed. I had no transportation to get to the medical school. Only one street car was running, and only on the main street. So I walked every day back and forth to classes, close to an hour each way. I spent much of my days studying in the library, as books to take home were not available. The food Father brought didn't last long. The family was not well organized and went through the supplies quickly. Father returned with more food which again disappeared just as fast. I often ate at the student cafeteria. Every day they served cabbage soup, which was mostly muddy-looking water with an occasional piece of cabbage floating in it. But in spite of all the hardships, I was very grateful to be able to study in Minsk.

Of all my teachers during that time, I especially remember the physics professor. Physics wasn't my favorite subject, but he made it interesting and enjoyable. It was in his class that I heard of Einstein's theory about splitting the atom for the first time. It sounded like a fairy tale to me.

One night a loud, aggressive knock on the main door woke up everyone in the little house I stayed in. Along with the family, I was terrified. It was the police, and they began searching the house; I had no idea what they were looking for. One of the policemen was an ex-partisan, and he started talking with me. He became polite and friendly, and said he knew some of the boys from Gleboki. In the end they arrested one of the daughters of the family housing us, but nobody ever told me why. I think she stole some food at work. The reason I'm including this incident here is that the way the police went about this – waking up people in the middle of the night in a very frightening and really terrorizing way – made it clear to me that once again I was living in a police state. It was just that right now, they weren't after me. Generally, the Russian people were friendly and good, though; it was the system that was bad.

To this day, I feel scared when I see police, even in the United States. My son always says to me, "Mom, there is no reason to fear the police. They are here to protect us." But this knowledge remains only in my head, while the rest of my body feels jittery and doomed as soon as any possibility of having to deal with policemen arises.

Another strong, very different feeling has stayed with me from those days: my love for opera. I saw the first opera of my life in Minsk; Carmen by Bizet. With its beautiful melodies and its passionate, tragic love story, it was a wonderful work to introduce me to the world of opera.

At the university, I met several people I became very fond of. One of them was a boy from Gleboki. He had enlisted in the Soviet Army as a volunteer and had lost both legs in the war. Now, an invalid at the age of nineteen, he studied law. He invited me to a dance, but couldn't dance.

There were very few young men on the streets of Minsk then, except the invalids, crippled for life. One day, when I was walking home on the main street, I heard a man screaming, "We were fighting! We have no place to live. The Abrams (Jews) didn't fight, and they get the apartments!" He was drunk, walking and yelling. This upset me very much and always stuck in my mind, as I knew many young Jews who fought in the war.

Another time, on a happier note, I ran into the red-haired partisan from the Boevoi Otriad with his "wife" Nina walking on that same street.

It was a great joy to see them, still together, in much more favorable circumstances than back in the woods.

At night, in the dark and abandoned streets of Minsk, a gang by the name of "The Black Cat" terrorized the people by robbing, killing, and torturing them.

Fortunately, anti-Semitism at the university was hidden. I personally never experienced it. However, the pressure of the Communist Party – "Komsomol" – was ever present. Interestingly enough, there was a market place in the middle of the city where one could buy almost anything – for a high price. It was illegal, but the government seemed to pay no attention to it. Actually, special stores existed for party officials while everyone else had to stand in line for hours. The party officials lived the good life in the best apartments of Minsk while the rest of the population struggled.

On the main street were several beauty shops. I used to do my own hair, but one day in the winter, just before New Year's, I decided to get a manicure. I waited in line in the manicure shop for many hours. Just when it was my turn, it was time for the shop to close. The manicurist felt sorry for me and gave me her address. She ran a private business in her home. When I arrived there, a crowd of women waited already in the one room she lived in. I had to wait for hours again. Luckily, a conversation ensued between me and a woman who was married to a high party official, and she took a liking to me. After she got her manicure, she asked the manicurist to give me my manicure next. I didn't have to wait any longer. This strikes me as an interesting story about human nature. There we were: no food, no light, no housing, no books to study from, no transportation, yet women waited for hours for a manicure. In my opinion it is a testament to the human spirit.

One evening, after a long day at the university, a lovely surprise was waiting for me in front of the little house I stayed in: Bomka! He had been transferred to Polotsk, a town in Eastern Belarus, about the same time I left for medical school. It was hard for him to take time off from work, but somehow he managed to get away. I was overjoyed and we spent a few cheerful days together. Usually nothing could distract me from my studies but, in this case, I was happy to leave the books closed other than during the scheduled classes. His visit was a special gift, especially since I knew how difficult it was for him to do it.

After my first semester, I went home to Gleboki for the winter vacation. There was much talk about leaving the Soviet Union. The former Polish citizens were allowed to go back to Poland. We wanted to go to Palestine to begin building our own country without anti-Semitism. Father didn't want to leave his hometown, but Mother and I didn't want to stay in the Soviet Union, along with most others in our community. Poland was to be just the first step in going to Palestine.

Father began changing his mind when he realized how the Soviets used the workers when they needed them, and got rid of them when they didn't. One day one of the party officials called Father into the office.

"What do you know about Irma Singer, the millionaire, the bourgeois?"

"My father was a very smart man. The Nazis killed him. If he was still alive and, if we had more people like him, we would have won the war much sooner."

After that conversation, we registered with the authorities to leave the Soviet Union. I continued my studies in Minsk until they called me to come home to begin our journey.

Chapter Eight

Since we had legal papers to leave the Soviet Union, we were able to bring our belongings with us to Poland. Bomka came with us, even though it was extremely difficult for him to quit his position in the government.

We traveled to Lodz by train with many other people who were returning to Poland. Most of them were farmers from Belarus. They were of Polish descent and, like us, had been Polish citizens before the war. They were unfriendly to us; they didn't like Jews and they showed it.

When we arrived in Lodz and took our belongings off the train, Uncle Moshe wanted me to escort the cow, which had traveled in one of the freight wagons. I refused.

"I am not going to walk in the City of Lodz with a cow," I said and stood my ground.

My family found an apartment in Lodz. Lodz felt strange and uncomfortable to me. The city had not been destroyed by the war, but the area where the ghetto used to be was completely devastated. Fortunately, we were only going to stay in Poland temporarily. We were determined to move on to Palestine to build our own country. Because we suffered so much during the Holocaust, we wanted to leave the place where we had lost family and friends. It was an effort to leave the bad memories behind and start a new life in our own country. Many people had begun the exodus to Palestine, which was difficult as the British, who maintained control over Palestine, severely restricted Jewish immigration, just like they had done during the war.

We joined a Kibbutz called "Gordonia." From the Kibbutz, boys and girls were sent to Western Europe and from there smuggled into Palestine. We were part of a big movement called the Aliyah Bet[5]. We kept our hopes up, even though we heard stories about how difficult the journey to our homeland was. Over ninety percent of the refugee ships were intercepted by the British Navy, and British authorities forced thousands of refugees off the ships into detention camps in Cyprus.

Since Boma (my nickname for Bomka, which was also a nickname for his real name Abraham) had an important government position in the Soviet Union, he was especially at risk in a Communist-ruled country like Poland. These boys were sent out west quickly. Boma asked me to go with him, but my parents forbade this unless we got married.

A Rabbi performed the ceremony. Boma needed two witnesses to attest that he hadn't been previously married. After the war many married people were separated from their spouses. The Rabbi wanted to make sure that this was not our case. It would not be acceptable for Boma to have a wife somewhere in the world and then to get married again. It seemed very funny to me – we were both so young, I used to say that we got married out of kindergarten. How could anyone think that Boma could have a wife somewhere else?

We also needed a couple of "Unterfierers" at our wedding, witnesses who had only been married once. It was hard to find such a couple, but my parents found a cousin who was lucky to have her first husband still alive and with her. It was rare because, during the war, many people lost husbands or wives. There was hardly a family left intact. I was very lucky to have my parents and my sister and often felt bad for Boma who had lost his entire family. The only person at the wedding from his side was Dr. Pliskin, who was also from Plissa. I believe he had survived in Russia. He was an important Zionist leader in Lodz and a very well-known person. Later, he went to Israel and became the mayor of Petach Tikva. With the little we had, my parents made a dinner for us to celebrate that Boma and I were now husband and wife.

This time, because we left illegally, we were not able to bring anything with us. We had to sell Boma's grandmother's silver by the pound, together with his mother's silver pocketbook. When I look back at my life, it amazes me how many times I had to leave a place without being

---

5 The code name given to illegal immigration by Jews to Palestine between 1934 and 1948

able to take my belongings and start a new life without anything tangible from the old life.

We left Lodz by train. Leaving my parents and Edith behind was incredibly sad. We had been through so much together and I knew I would miss them terribly, which I did. Yet I was also excited to embark on this journey with my husband. When I hugged Mother, Father, and Edith goodbye, I kept telling myself that Boma and I were paving the way for them to follow us soon. That eased the painful farewell a little bit.

A man from the Brichah escorted us to Stettin (Szczecin), a Pomeranian port city on the Baltic Sea. Brichah was the organization that arranged the Aliyah Bet exodus to Palestine from Eastern Europe. In Stettin we met a big group of mostly young people. Many of them had escaped from the Soviet Union. We all had to hide in a house so nobody would see us. Finally, in the dark of the night, we were ushered onto a truck which was supposed to deliver milk across the border to Eastern Germany. Even though there was no light in the truck and I couldn't see the others' faces, I felt their tension as well as mine. Nobody spoke a word. When the truck stopped and we heard men's voices speaking German with our driver, we knew we were at the border. Everybody seemed to hold their breath. Seconds felt like hours. What would happen if, instead of milk cans, the border police found a group of young Zionists huddled in the back of the truck? Luckily, the guards did not inspect the cargo and before long the truck rumbled on.

When we arrived in Berlin, they brought us to the French zone. After the war, Berlin had been divided into four zones: American, British, French, and Russian. We stayed in Berlin for about two weeks. Boma and I shared a tiny bed. I had to wash and dry our only outfits.

Berlin in 1946 was practically destroyed. It reminded me of Minsk. Being a medical student seemed like a very long time ago though it had only been a few months before. Now I was a married fugitive.

I wanted to see the Reichstag, the Nazi government building. It had been bombed to the ground and was in the Russian zone. We took the subway which, interestingly, still functioned well. Seeing the Reichstag in ruins was a grand moment which I will never forget. All the evil that we and millions of others experienced came from this terrible place. To see it decimated now gave me great satisfaction, yet it struck me that there was also something unpleasant about seeing any ruins.

In Berlin we met Israeli soldiers for the first time. They were actually Jewish soldiers in the British Brigade from what was then still called Palestine. They came to our Kibbutz and sang Israeli songs and danced the Horah. It was so much fun and very uplifting. They reminded me of the Russian soldiers. We also saw French soldiers in a coffeehouse near us. The French looked and behaved differently; they all seemed to be very playful.

After a couple of weeks, we were given passports to continue our journey west. All of us took the train together, but we were instructed to spread out and not be too obvious. The train was comfortable by comparison to the awful Russian trains I took going to Minsk. It was a long journey from Berlin to Munich and we traveled toward the American zone in southwestern Germany.

When we were about to enter the American zone, we were stopped and had to get off the train to go through a checkpoint. There was a line of thousands of people trying to go west. Some of them waited for days. I didn't realize that I was experiencing history in the making. Thinking back on it, this truly was such a historical time. It was an amazing movement of displaced people across Europe.

We passed the checkpoint and got back on the train. In Heidelberg the train was stopped and everyone had to get off again. This was the first time that I saw American soldiers – Military Police – and the first time I saw a black person in my life. The MPs were manning the checkpoint. Most people were waved through, but some were questioned and searched.

When it was my turn, the MP stopped me. I saw the others from my group go through without difficulty. I was terrified. In retrospect, I understand why it happened. It was summertime, yet I wore a fur collar around my coat. Boma had given it to me as a present and I had thought, if I was wearing it, I could take it with me. But a blond woman wearing fur around her neck on a sunny summer day, of course, arose the American soldiers' suspicion. They probably assumed that I was a Nazi trying to escape. Fortunately the leader of the Brichah came to my rescue and the Americans let me through. I was still shaken when we got on another train and continued our journey.

Our next destination was a displaced persons camp in Deggendorf, a small town in the American zone of Bavaria. There were mostly older Jewish people from Austria and Hungary in this camp. We were supposed to wait indefinitely, until a boat would take us to Palestine. It was such a waste to me, just to sit around and wait. I missed my family and my studies desperately, lost my appetite, and became more and more depressed.

I knew that Aunt Celia – Father's younger sister who had married Uncle Velvel in Golducha and had given birth there to little Soraleh – lived in another DP camp, in Föhrenwald, about an hour from Munich. So I asked my leader for permission to go to Munich. Since we were able to travel freely in the American zone, Boma and I got on a train again. Aunt Celia and Uncle Velvel and little Soraleh were very happy to see us. They also had a new addition to the family, a baby girl named Miriam.

A student lived next door to them who told me about the Jewish Student Union in Munich. I got excited about the possibility of continuing my studies. Very quickly Boma and I decided to remain in Föhrenwald and enrolled at the UNRAA (United Nations Rehabilitation and Relief Agency) University, a university for refugees. And to our great joy, Mother, Father, Edith, Aunt Ella, and little Asya, who'd moved from Lodz to Vienna after Boma and I left, soon came to Föhrenwald as well. Once again, life felt bright with real hope for a better future to me. Being united with my loved ones and able to go back to university made feeling optimistic easy for me, despite the terrible stories we heard about thousands of people who were turned back from Palestinian shores after grueling journeys in overcrowded ships.

Asya's father, who was a poor man before he married Aunt Ella, had traveled a lot and gone to Palestine before the war. He had asked Aunt Ella for a divorce from there. Initially, she refused him, but Father talked to her, and eventually she signed the divorce papers. So now, Asya had the opportunity to go to Palestine legally, because of her father. Asya soon left while Aunt Ella remained with my parents in Föhrenwald. But Asya didn't get along with her father and his new wife and before long got married to a young soldier. Aunt Ella followed her later when Israel became independent.

Cousin Mira – I don't remember when we finally found out what had happened to her – was also able to move to Palestine legally, because her parents lived there. Mira had survived several camps, as had her husband, Sima, the young doctor. Sima even lived through one of the death marches. But Mira's life remained difficult. Sima became strange after the war. He was brilliant, and he threw himself into his work as a research scientist. They were in Jerusalem, and during the War of Independence, Mira was among those who were cut off and went without food in the old city, while he was at the Hadassah Hospital, not suffering hunger. And when they realized they couldn't have children, Mira wanted to adopt. It was easy to adopt in those days, as there were many children who had lost their parents. But Sima didn't want to. Mira ended up working as a nurse pretty much her entire life, and they did eventually have a beautiful apartment in Jerusalem.

Aunt Hannah and Uncle Moshe went from Lodz to Krakow, where they were reunited with their younger son Elusha. Eventually they made their way to another DP camp in Germany – Bad Windsheim. They were still mourning the loss of their older son.

It was also finally confirmed that Uncle Lipa's entire family had been murdered. My grandfather's brother, his wife, his four sons, Aunt Bertha from Riga, and Cousin Gita – she'd been four months younger than I and we used to play together in our beautiful home in Vilno – they were all dead. It was only because Father was always one step ahead of the Nazis that we had survived, and even with all his wisdom, Father had not been able to save his parents and Uncle Mula who were shot during the slaughter in Gleboki Ghetto. I still missed my grandparents terribly. And, of course, my poor Boma had lost his entire family. But we talked very little about the past and about our losses. We all dealt with the grief by ourselves in our own way, I suppose.

As soon as my parents arrived in Föhrenwald, Mother began working in the hospital, on the maternity ward. Many, many babies were born in DP camps in those days, and there were more men than women in our population, as more women and children had been killed during the war. Edith applied at an ORT-school, a Jewish organization that taught people trades. She soon began studying to be a dental technician. Föhrenwald was a self-governing camp and there was an election. Most people who ran for office belonged to the Zionist labor parties. Father, who had always been a businessman, started a new party which represented the middle class. He won the election and gained a seat in the "Verwaltung", the camp administration. We were so proud of him. Little did we know that soon something would happen that changed everything once again, and not for the better.

Chapter Nine

IN THE SUMMER OF 1946, Boma and I moved to Munich to begin our studies at the university. It was extremely difficult to find a place to live because the city was overcrowded. After much searching, we found a room on the fourth floor of an apartment building on Robert-Koch-Strasse. There was no elevator, of course. The building was located in the heart of the city, with easy access to public transport and in walking distance to museums, theaters, a wonderful park named the English Garden, and the River Isar. I loved going for walks on the beautiful river banks, especially in the fall when the chestnuts fell from the trees. A Nazi had formerly owned this apartment He had to vacate and it now belonged to a working man and his wife and small son. They had their own big kitchen and sublet rooms to students who shared a kitchenette. We all shared one bathroom.

Initially, we lived in a small room in the middle of the apartment. Two German men shared the bigger corner room. One of them was a Nazi. He was a physics teacher and ever so charming. He even helped me with my studies. One afternoon a friend of mine, a pharmacy student who also had trouble with physics, joined me to study. We got talking, and he complained to us about German women. His wife had left him for an American.

"German women are the worst," he said. "They're not like the French, Belgian, and Polish women who are devoted to their husbands."

"It's your upbringing," my friend said. I was quiet. In a way, I even felt sorry for him.

"What do you mean?" he asked her.

"You believe that the toughest and strongest are the best." She let him have it. "Now that Americans are stronger than the Germans, your wife did what she was taught. She left the weak behind and went with the stronger one."

He moved out not long after we moved in. The other fellow suggested that Boma and I should take the bigger room with the two windows, since he was by himself now. It was still in the summer, so we didn't realize that the windows needed to be fixed and the heat wasn't working. Once winter arrived, the room became freezing cold. We ended up sleeping in the tiny kitchenette we shared with the German student while he was cozy in his small, centrally located room. Thankfully, the gas stove in the little kitchen where we cooked our meals kept us warm.

In spite of the crowding, people we knew from the DP camp stayed with us when they came to Munich. Edith practically lived with us much of the time. We never refused anyone who asked to stay with us. However, they had to sleep in the bed in our cold room. Elusha – Aunt Hannah and Uncle Moshe's son – grew impatient sitting around waiting for passage to Palestine in the DP camp in Bad Windsheim, so he came to Munich and looked for a job. He acquired a position in public relations at a Jewish organization and stayed with us until he found a room to rent. Elusha never complained about being cold in the drafty corner room without heat, even though he was with us in the winter. The following year, we purchased a small iron stove which was heated with coal. We bought coal across the street and had to haul it ourselves from the cellar to the fourth floor. In the spring, all was forgotten.

Immediately after we moved in, I began my studies at the UNRAA University. However, at the end of the summer, the UNRRA University was closed. Fortunately, the students who belonged to the Jewish Student Union were granted permission to register at German universities. I began attending the Ludwig Maximilians University, one of the oldest and most famous universities in Germany. Mira wrote to me from Israel – which was still Palestine – and told me that Israel had too many physicians and not so many dentists. She suggested that I study dentistry instead. Boma, who took classes in engineering, thought that, as a dentist, I would spend more time at home than if I became a physician and had to work nights in the hospital. So I decided to study dentistry instead of medicine.

The Jewish Student Union was an important part of our life in Munich. When I went to the Student Union building for the first time,

I saw a piano in the corner. I walked over to it and played a piece by Chopin that I still knew by heart from when I was a child. A young woman approached me.

"I used to know a girl who played this song all the time. Back in Vilno."

I stopped playing and glanced up at her. She looked familiar.

"I'm from Vilno," I said.

"Asya!" she exclaimed. "You're that girl!"

Her name was Ala. She was friends with my cousin, Gita, who I grew up with in the Singer House. So much had happened to us since we were children.

The students were from many different countries and backgrounds: Most came from Poland, others from Hungary, Germany, Russia, Lithuania, Czechoslovakia, and the Ukraine; some had been fighting in the Russian army; some had been partisans; others had lived undercover with Aryan papers, or were hidden by courageous non-Jews; some came from Siberian labor camps; the largest majority were survivors of concentration camps. Ages varied as well. Some students were older, had started a university education before the war and had been interrupted. Others had studied in the Soviet Union during the war. Boma and I were among the younger students. But we all had the same goal: to study and graduate with a diploma.

We were a highly motivated and tight-knit group. Often we got together for lunch in a cafeteria for Jewish students, on Isartorplatz, a lively place where we'd meet and socialize. Boys met girls and vice versa. Many got married. Some, like Boma and I, were married already. We also had student dances which were a lot of fun. Almost never did we speak about our past. Only with one's closest friends did one feel free to talk about the Holocaust and his or her experience, and even that very rarely. We all survived a terrible time and had started a new life. We felt like we were reborn.

The Student Union organized many wonderful trips. We went boating in the summer and skiing in the winter. Boma was always athletic whereas I was not. I was a beginner and didn't have good skis and, even after several skiing trips, I remained a beginner. The evenings were filled with much cheer, singing, and socializing, so I nevertheless enjoyed myself.

I became good friends with Henia, whom I knew from Svencionys. She was two years older than I and had graduated high school in 1941. Henia remembered my father's generosity. During the time when Father worked in Lyntupy and we still lived in Gleboki, he rented a hotel room in Svencionys. Henia was from a tiny town that didn't have a school, so she shared a room with a girlfriend in Svencionys. This girl liked to play around and have fun, whereas Henia was of the studious sort, like me. Somehow, Father got to know Henia. He let her use his hotel room during the day while he was at work, so she could get away from her noisy roommate and concentrate on her studies. Henia was a medical student now and actually lived in the building next to us on Robert-Koch-Strasse. Her husband, Mark Liebhaber, was an editor of a Jewish magazine. Whenever I had a headache, Boma said I should go over there for a chat and my headache would be gone. Most of the time it worked. Little did I know that one day, when they left for America, we would live in their quarters, which was larger than ours.

Once Boma and I went skiing with two other guys. It was a daytrip, not organized by the Student Union. Munich is close to the Alps. We took the lift up and the view was breathtaking. But there was no way I was going to ski down those slopes. So I went to the café, had a hot chocolate, and admired the mountains. The sky was bright blue, and the snow sparkled in the sun like someone had sprinkled diamond dust on the ground. When the sun disappeared behind the mountains, I took the lift back down. It was almost dark when I got to the parking lot. The guys weren't there yet. I sat in the car and watched more and more cars drive away. Soon the parking lot was almost empty, but my boys were nowhere to be seen. I got very worried. Finally I asked some people if anything unusual had happened.

"Yes," they said, "a foreigner had an accident."

I was sure it was Boma who was in trouble. It seemed like an eternity until they showed up, and I was so relieved that my husband was walking without even a limp. The mountain paramedics carried our friend, Hillel, to the car, and then we took him to Munich to the Jewish hospital. He had broken his leg and needed to stay in the hospital for a while.

It was strange how we ended up living in Germany among Germans, the country and the people who wanted to destroy us. When I first came to Munich, I resented every German and everything that surrounded me. So we kept our distance.

One day, I was going home on a streetcar, when suddenly a woman I didn't know approached me. She was the wife of the Nazi who had owned the apartment where we lived. We paid our rent to the new owner. She obviously thought we had to pay rent to her. She stopped me and said, "You Jews are on the black market – Sie sind alle Schwarzhändler!" I was caught by surprise, speechless and frozen. When I arrived home I was very upset and told Boma.

He walked over to her house and warned her never to attack me in public again.

She said, "You were not in a concentration camp."

Boma replied, "You won't live long enough to put me in a concentration camp. I will put you in a concentration camp!" and walked out. This was Bomka after all, the famous partisan who wouldn't take anything from anybody.

But most people were civil to me, and over time, I became fond of the city. It wasn't too large or too small, just right, and it had a lot of charm and warmth, so-called "Gemütlichkeit."

We went to Föhrenwald regularly to visit the family; the hour train ride was comfortable, and there were Jewish taxis. The drivers would wait until they filled up the car from the train station in Wolfratshausen to Föhrenwald and back. Mother gave us food to take home when we returned to Munich. Food was scarce and we didn't have much money to buy it on the black market. All residents of the DP camp received a monthly package. Father, as an elected official, made it his business to fight for the students to also receive the package. He won and the privilege was granted. The cigarettes we received from our monthly package paid our rent, and the coffee paid for much of our food.

Alice Singer-Genis with Emunah Herzog

Mother, Father, Edith, Bomka and I in Föhrenwald. Germany (1946)

Me in the German Alps. Berchtesgaden (1948)

I used to do business with our neighbor; she was a single woman and quite funny once she warmed up to me. I sold her my coffee. Just as we kept our distance, the Germans were suspicious of us as well in the beginning. We were foreigners, not just Jews. But after a while they saw that we didn't steal, weren't noisy or drunks, so they relaxed and interactions became quite friendly.

"Wir sind resolute Frauen (we are resolute women)," she'd say to me and we'd laugh together. "When my sister comes to visit, I won't give her this coffee," she'd say. "I'll give her Ersatz Kaffee (fake coffee)."

Another woman in the building brought me a plate for bread with Hebrew writing on it one day. "Someone gave it to me," she said. "I want you to have it."

On the corner of our street was a butcher store, a "Metzgerei." In the beginning, the meat was rationed. They had schnitzels there and other parts of meat that was neatly cut and looked appetizing. I used to buy there occasionally. The Germans complained that they didn't get enough food. But looking at the standard of living of Germany, who had lost the war, and Russia, who had won the war, there was no comparison. I knew this from firsthand experience, especially from living in Minsk. The German standard of living, even with the food shortage, was much higher than in the Soviet Union at that time.

I fondly remember the Roman baths in Munich with their smooth marble floors, a beautiful, sparkling pool, and even a steam room. We had no tub or shower and only one toilet for all who lived in the apartment. I used to wash myself in a basin. But once a week we would go to the Roman baths which cost very little and felt luxurious. Especially in the wintertime the showers with their seemingly endless supply of hot water were such a delight.

We also enjoyed the cultural life of Munich. For only two "Reichsmarks", students could buy theater and opera tickets to performances that hadn't sold out. The "Theater der Jugend" (Theater for the Youth) was close to where we lived. Even closer was "Die kleine Komödie" (The Little Comedy). Both were excellent theaters. We saw several Shakespeare plays there among other very good plays. And it was wonderful for me to deepen my love for opera which had begun in Minsk.

A magnificent art museum – the "Haus der Kunst" – was walking distance from us as well. My friend, Hillel Klein, the one who broke his leg skiing, knew much about art. He would go with me and explain the paintings and sculptures to me. I was overwhelmed; there was so much beauty. It was like I was transformed. The Haus der Kunst was my first exposure to art. Later in my life we traveled extensively, both in America and in Europe, and I went to museums everywhere. To this day, wherever I go, I like to visit the museums.

On Sundays, when we didn't visit Föhrenwald, Boma, Edith, and I often went to the zoo, or for long walks in Munich's beautiful park, the English Garden. Before long, Boma and Elusha bought a car together, a black, shiny Citroen. They took turns driving it. Unfortunately, the Citroen turned out to be unreliable. I remember being dressed up to go to the theater, and the car wouldn't start. Edith and I had to push it with all our might while Boma sat in the driver's seat turning the ignition and releasing the clutch when we had gained enough momentum. Once I wore new shoes – red suede pumps that had cost me a fortune and were hard to come by – and the oil from the Citroen ruined them. Our next car was a DKW, a tiny car that still makes me smile when I think of it. It took us up, up, up the mountains on many wonderful trips. I don't remember why we got rid of it. The last car we had in Munich was an old Mercedes that Boma got secondhand for a good price. Boma loved his cars and chauffeured everyone wherever they needed to go with great pleasure. I knew that I was very lucky to have my parents, my sister and, of course, my husband. Most people in the Jewish Student Union didn't have what I had. However, my luck didn't last long.

I remember the day Mother walked into the apartment in Robert-Koch-Strasse, tears streaming down her face, as if it was yesterday.

"Father died," she said, sobbing. I simply couldn't believe it and took her into our room.

He was having problems with his prostate, and a doctor Mother worked with had suggested a hospital in the outskirts of Munich where they had cured this doctor's prostate disease. So Mother took Father there. There was an American doctor who said to operate right away, but the German doctor in charge was against an operation. They argued and didn't make up their mind while Father lay in his hospital bed and Mother was busy with work and we with our studies. We had no idea it was that serious.

The year before, just after my parents arrived in Föhrenwald from Poland, Father had gone to the hospital for a skin problem. A young doctor had diagnosed him with hemorrhoids and talked Father into an operation.

"There's nothing to it," the enthusiastic young medical man had said to Father. "I'll take them out and you won't suffer any more."

But Father acquired an infection and suffered for quite some time, as there were no antibiotics available. Eventually he was well again and discharged from the hospital. It was inconceivable that he was dead now.

As if in a trance, I went to Edith's school and got her to step out of the classroom. Her eyes were big and she looked so very young.

"I have bad news," I said to her. "Father died."

At first Edith didn't want to believe me.

"How can this be?" she said. "I visited him last night. He was talking. He looked like he was feeling better. How can this be?"

When we arrived in the hospital, his body was in the morgue already.

His face looked so beautiful, so peaceful, but his abdomen was very swollen. Over the years I often felt that perhaps we could have done more for him, visited more often, stayed with him. Maybe he would have been better off in the Jewish hospital where they had some antibiotics. Had we known how serious it was, we would have dropped everything to be with him. The thought of him dying by himself in the hospital room still hurts me deeply.

It was a terrible, terrible loss for us. For months, I felt the grief as a physical pain in my whole body. I'd almost always been able to look at the bright side of things quickly again after bad things happened to us. In the ghetto, I had made the best of the situation chatting with my friends while grinding beets in the jam factory. Even during the harsh life in the woods, I saw the beauty of nature and came up with enjoyable things to dream about. But now, over and over again, I felt as if I were leaning against a wall that crumbled, leaving me with nothing to support me. My father, the young, strong man, who had been full of vitality and who we could always count on, was no longer. My security was gone. Of course Mother and Edith felt this enormous loss deeply, too. We had lost our leader.

Nochem Singer, the great and kind man who had been our rock, was buried in the new section of the Jewish cemetery in Munich. I remember the cemetery well. It was remarkable that it had not been destroyed by the Nazi regime. On the contrary, it was well kept and looked cared for. We picked a beautiful gravestone and planted a tree above it. Edith and I visited quite often and brought flowers. We missed our father so much. We got to know the German couple that took care of the cemetery. They were friendly people, paid by the Jewish community. The old part of the cemetery looked like a park with beautiful tall trees and flowers. I was happily surprised to see it, remembering how destroyed the Jewish cemeteries were in Russia and Poland.

Mother took the nightshift as a midwife at the hospital, because she couldn't sleep. Aunt Ella kept her company during the day and Aunt Celia tried to comfort Mother as well. As often as we could, we went to Föhrenwald on the weekends to be together.

I threw myself into my studies. I had always been an efficient and conscientious student, but now I studied harder than ever. The dental and medical students had our lectures together in a big auditorium. The laboratory was separate for the dental students. I liked the theory better than the labs. I usually studied with boys. There was only one other Jewish girl in my class. She studied alone, whereas I preferred to study together with another person.

For my state board exam, I studied with a man who, at the time of this writing, is retired and lives in Israel. He became a very successful dentist in Tel Aviv, as is his son. I also studied with a medical student who became a wonderful doctor and still practices in Chicago. My good friend, Hillel Klein, became a well known psychiatrist who lived in Israel and lectured all over the world.

Boma had started to study engineering, but when I was in dental school, I realized how important dexterity was for this profession. He had always been very handy and bright. He accepted my suggestion to switch to dentistry and became an excellent dentist. Our fellow students from Munich turned into successful physicians, engineers, economists, and dentists all over the world. One was in the German parliament, others in the Israeli governments. Some went into business, others became Rabbis. Deep friendships were formed and we kept in touch by having reunions and through a yearly news publication. The last reunion was in Israel in 2006.

It took a while after Father died, but eventually we convinced Mother to join Edith, Boma, and me on trips into the Alps. We also started traveling with a friend of hers, Dr. Steiman, and his family. The Steimans had a beautiful big car, but our little DKW kept up with them nicely, even on the mountain roads. Sometimes we traveled in a caravan of several cars. Mother went with us to the Zugspitze, the highest peak in Germany. We also visited the many famous castles built by Prince Ludwig of Bavaria. I got to travel a fair amount in Germany. I saw Frankfurt am Main, Würzburg, Heidelberg, amongst other German towns in the American zone, which was free. The freedom was palpable, especially after what we had experienced in the Soviet Union.

One day, Mother told us that she was going to travel to the United States. The hospital in Föhrenwald needed nurses to escort refugees on their journeys to America. So Mother took a job on a ship to visit her two sisters and her brother who had gone to America long before the war. When the ship arrived in Boston, all of her family came to pick her up. They were very warm and friendly, she told me when she returned. We started talking about perhaps going to America instead of Palestine and registered for immigration to the United States.

When we filed our papers, we were told that our Ketubah – the religious document of marriage – wasn't sufficient, so we got married again in the City Hall in Wolfratshausen. We didn't know we would need two witnesses, so Boma approached two Bavarian men who gladly helped us out. It must have been a funny sight, Boma and I with two guys in Lederhosen[6]! Many of our friends applied for immigration to several countries, but just because one had registered did not mean one was accepted. Others took chances on being smuggled into Palestine. I had already made it clear that I wasn't going to Palestine illegally before I completed my studies. I was not going to take a chance on ending up in a camp on Cyprus and have my education interrupted for the third time. But Boma and I were very involved in the Zionist movement. We stayed informed and the hope for Israel to be officially ours became more and more realistic, yet when it came to pass, it was hard to believe that it was happening.

During exuberant celebrations many tears of joy were shed, but our happiness was short-lived. When Arabs attacked Israel from all sides, we felt threatened to the core. I remember going to a student meeting where people were called to immediately go to help. Few were willing to do that. Most of our students were pro-Israel, but didn't want to go now. One student said that, if it wasn't for the Nüremberg Laws, he wouldn't consider himself Jewish. We were all very disturbed by this remark. I wanted to continue my studies, graduate, and then go. So did most other students and many did just that after graduation. But a few volunteered right away. I remember one young man; he was the brother of a student, a lively fellow with red hair and shining brown eyes. He left and was killed in 1948.

Cousin Aryeh, who had told me Boma's heroic stories over and over again in the woods, also volunteered immediately. He was a young boy, sixteen or seventeen now, younger than Edith. As soon as he arrived in Israel he went into the army to fight. Later we heard how difficult the situation was for them, how they had no guns and went back and forth between the different borders to defend our homeland. To this day, I am

---

6 Leather shorts

amazed at how they managed to win. Aryeh is a retired colonel today, struggling with health problems.

1948 also brought big changes to Germany. A currency reform was enacted and, as soon as the money was changed to the new "Währung", everything changed with it. Munich felt like a different city. Suddenly the stores were full of everything, from food to clothing to leather goods to jewelry. The restaurants and coffee houses began to reopen. The theaters and movie houses were full of patrons. Everyone was given twenty-five Deutschmarks and the old money became worthless. What did Edith and I do with our first new money? We went to the opera.

Soon my life changed again, too. I graduated from the university in 1949, after working very hard for my state board exam. It was an amazing feeling to hold my diploma in my hands. If only Father could have been there. I was very proud to be a "Zahnärztin", a dentist. For a short while, I worked at the Freiman DP camp, just outside of Munich, but it soon closed down. And, I became pregnant. Boma was still a student at the time and also worked as a truck driver.

It was then that we were called for an interview regarding immigration to America and we decided, if we were accepted, that's where we were going to go. It was a difficult decision and there were several reasons why we came to it: Aside from the hostile neighbors surrounding Israel, we heard how difficult the economic situation was. Without Father we still felt hurt and lost and not really up to facing such a challenge. Many countries began opening their doors to Jewish refugees such as Australia, Canada, South America, and the U.S.A. We wanted to go to a democratic and free country like the U.S.A. Since we had family in the States, it seemed to be the right place for us.

We had no problems being granted permission. Many applicants were rejected for various reasons. We were lucky to be young, strong, and educated people. When we went to see the consul, I was visibly pregnant. I still remember that Boma wore shorts, a habit he had picked up from the Bavarians. The officials asked Boma some questions. He answered them honestly and directly. This was the way he was and people liked him for it. So was I. I always was myself and never pretended to be someone or something I'm not. But they never asked me any questions. It still took a couple of years between the interview and our actual departure.

My little boy was born in Föhrenwald. Mother kept me in her

apartment which was across from the hospital where she worked until I was almost ready to give birth.

"Women always come too early to the hospital," she said.

To me it felt like it took forever. Another midwife came to be with us. Finally we went to the hospital. Giving birth naturally was very painful, but at least I knew the doctor who attended to me; he was a friend of my mother's. The whole staff gave me much attention and I had a bright, comfortable room. As soon as my baby was born, all the hardship was forgotten. What a lovely little boy our baby was. We named him Nathan after Father. But because he was so cute, everybody called him Pipsi.

When we were discharged from the hospital, we stayed with Mother. The baby was beautiful, but we noticed that something was wrong with his breathing. He also couldn't take the breast or the bottle. The doctor told me to have the baby seen at the children's hospital in Munich. The diagnosis was that Pipsi had been born with a congenital heart defect.

Poor Pipsi was hospitalized for a long time. I went to the hospital every day. He had his own room. Because he had such a hard time breathing, they always kept the windows open. It was fall and already quite cold outside, but he was well covered. The nurses were nuns and calm and efficient. The professor checked the baby often. I was always there. The professor told me not to stay in the cold because I would get sick soon, too. Finally we were able to take Pipsi home. He needed a lot of care so we got him a baby nurse.

Fortunately, at that time, my friend Henia from Svencionys and her husband, Mark, left for America and gave us their quarters. So we now had two rooms in the building attached to ours and didn't have to leave the part of the city I liked so much. The landlady, Frau von Natusius, was an old, odd woman. She lived in the apartment with her daughter, who always seemed like an old maid to me. Frau von Natasius had been a landowner in East Germany. The Communists had taken everything away from her, but she was lucky that she owned this apartment in Bavaria. She still behaved like she was her ladyship and thought that one day her estate would be returned to its rightful owner. In addition to us, she rented rooms to a family of four from East Germany and to a Greek man. We all cooked in one big kitchen. In our old apartment, I had cooked in the tiny kitchenette, but I was the only one to cook there; the other student only came in occasionally to make his coffee. I brought my own gas stove, which made things easier, and Frau von Natusius and the other woman shared one stove. Once again, we all shared one bathroom. But it was helpful to have a second room now that we had the sick baby and his nurse.

I didn't like the nurse much; she was a real know-it-all and not a warm person. I cherished Sundays, when she was off. One of my favorite things to do was to take Pipsi in his baby carriage to the English Garden, which was walking distance from Robert-Koch-Strasse. He was a beautiful and very good baby, with soft brown hair and hazel eyes that became so big when he struggled for air. It was extremely painful to see my baby suffer and sometimes I felt very, very helpless. We went to see the professor from the children's hospital regularly.

Another great sadness descended on us: Uncle Velvel suddenly died in his sleep from a heart attack. Now it was Mother who had to comfort Aunt Celia and help her take care of her two little girls.

In 1950, Mother and Edith were called to go to America and soon left, as did Aunt Celia and her daughters.

Boma accompanied Mother and Edith to the train, which was to take them to Bremen, where they would board the ship. The train station was filled with displaced people leaving to go to America. Boma ran into a fellow student and introduced them. Amos had graduated from the Technische Hochschule and was an engineer. I remember dancing with Amos at student dances.

"Amos is a nice guy," Boma said to Mother and Edith. "He'll help you with your luggage. Right, Amos?"

Amos nodded. They had no idea how important this moment was.

Amos was born in Israel, but his parents couldn't get used to the living conditions in the Middle-East and returned to Poland when Amos was a baby in the twenties. His mother was killed in Auschwitz; his father was one of the few people who survived Auschwitz. Amos somehow managed to pass as a non-Jewish Polish worker in Silesia, at that time part of Germany. He came eerily close to being found out by a German doctor, but either this man failed to notice that Amos was circumcised, or he pretended not to notice. No one will ever know.

In Bremen, Amos and Edith went sightseeing together, and during the sea voyage they spent a lot of time with each other and fell in love. But Amos was headed for Chicago, while Edith went with Mother to New

York. Eventually Edith moved to Chicago and got married to Amos, and they are still a happy couple.

Fortunately, when Mother and Edith left Munich, Pipsi was doing a little bit better. Boma was studying hard for his state board exam and worked at a clinic. I spent much time with Pipsi.

Something beautiful happened to Boma. He went to the Jewish center on Mell-Strasse one day, I don't remember why. At the center he met a young man who had just returned from Stockholm. The two of them got engaged in a conversation. The young man told Boma about his trip, and the "heymische" bed-and-breakfast where he stayed, run by a Jewish woman from Poland. She was a hard working woman and did it all by herself, the young man said. When he mentioned her name, Boma couldn't believe his ears. Could it be that this was his Aunt Liba, his father's sister? He had only met her once, when he was still a child and she came for a visit to Poland. He wrote a letter to her and, indeed, it was her. It was such a great happiness for Boma to find a living family member after all, and she had grown children, a daughter and a son. She soon came for a visit to Munich and we had a delightful time. We traveled to Berchtesgaden and to the salt mines together. I still have a picture from those happy days.

Toward the end of 1950, around Christmas time, Boma's Aunt Liba invited him to visit her. He needed a special permit, which she got for him. So I was alone with Pipsi in Munich. I remember taking a walk in the evening on Christmas Eve. The streets were empty; everybody was with their family. I stopped on Stacchus and looked at a window decoration when somebody came over and asked me if I cared to spend the evening with an American soldier. I said, "No, thank you," and quickly got into the Strassenbahn and went home.

And then, in 1951, we too were called to go to America. I told the professor, Pipsi's pediatrician, about our plans. Did he think Pipsi could take the trip? He said that going by plane would be the fastest and easiest way for the baby to travel. We applied for permission to go by plane with the baby. They gave us permission eventually. In the meantime Boma still had to finish his semester and take the state board exam.

Everybody had to move to a transition camp called Von-Kaserne in order to go to America. When we were called, Boma still had one exam to take to get his diploma. He told me to go to speak to the man in charge and ask for a postponement to the next transit by plane. It wasn't easy to get this. I didn't know how to approach him. I pretended to be the scared little woman and told the man that I was afraid of what my husband would do if we had to leave before he was finished with his exam. So the man put us on the list for the next plane, a month or so later.

Aunt Liba, Boma's aunt from Stockholm, came to say good bye before we left. I was happy that a member of Boma's family bid us farewell from Europe, since he had lost all of his loved ones.

Somehow Boma met the man in charge of the transition camp who was from Belarus. When he saw this "Landsmann", they had a drink together, then another drink, then another. After many, many drinks, the Belarusian told Boma that we didn't have to stay in the transition camp. We could come directly to the airport, which was a big help to us with the sick baby. I still went to Frau von Natusius to pay our rent. Aunt Liba couldn't get over how my husband came home, very drunk, and I paid the rent. I'll never forget when she said to Boma, "With a wife like this, you can go to the end of the world."

Chapter Ten

EVEN THOUGH WE WERE AMONG the fortunate ones to make our passage from Europe to America in an airplane instead of on a ship, it was an arduous journey.

We were ushered into an old army plane which was packed to the brim with parents and small children. People came from all different places; mostly from the Ukraine, Lithuania, and other East European countries including East Germany. It was terribly noisy: The old engines roared, the rickety overhead bins rattled, little children screamed nonstop, and adults had to shout at each other to make themselves heard. We stopped twice, once in Ireland and once in Iceland, where we were allowed to get off the plane.

My poor Pipsi suffered so much, it was heartbreaking. He struggled for each breath, his hazel eyes huge and fearful. While everybody around us was so noisy, he was incredibly quiet. I tried to comfort him best I could. All the passengers near us said what a good baby he was and he truly was. But the journey was very, very hard on him.

When we finally arrived in New York, Mother and Edith were waiting for us. The joy we felt to be together again! I'm sure each of us also experienced the pain of not having Father with us, but we didn't mention it.

Going through immigration and dealing with the Jewish organizations at the airport took hours. After we completed the last piece of paperwork, Mother and Edith took us to our apartment in Queens.

Excited, they led us into the apartment which was on the ground floor of a rather new building. They had lived with Mother's sister in Brooklyn in the beginning. Mother had started working as a nurse at Kew Gardens

Hospital right away and soon found a job for Edith in Medical Records. Finding an apartment had been difficult, but eventually they obtained this one in Queens. Initially Dr. Steiman – Mother's friend from Munich – and his family had lived in the second bedroom but, fortunately, they found a place of their own just before we arrived.

Even though it was a simple two-bedroom apartment with a tiny kitchen – more of a kitchenette which was common in New York in those days – it was beautiful. Mother and Edith had done such a wonderful job decorating it. Mother's taste had always been impeccable. For the living room they had bought a modern couch and an elegant lamp. Edith had found a bookcase in the garbage and hauled it to the apartment and painted it green. It was ever so attractive. They put a table and chairs into the entrance hall, which from then on functioned beautifully as the dining room. We ate many meals there together, both happy and sad. Mother and Edith slept in one bedroom, Boma, Pipsi, and I in the other. All Boma and I had to buy was a bedroom set which I still remember; it cost us $300 and was reddish mahogany.

Like probably every other new immigrant to America, I was overwhelmed by how big the stores were and how much was available. It took me a while to get used to it. I fondly remember a fish store that was close to our apartment. I would go there and buy a whole flounder. It was inexpensive, because it still had the bones, and it was absolutely delicious. We had a washer and a dryer in the basement. Dryers were unheard of in those days in Europe! And sometimes we took our laundry to the Chinese laundry, which cost very little and felt luxurious. Over the years I have often heard it said that New Yorkers are rude, but I've always found them to be friendly people.

Boma had studied English at the Hebrew Gymnasium in Vilno and in his easygoing way talked with everybody right away. I think he developed this ability by living among strangers since he graduated elementary school and it helped him tremendously throughout his entire life. He had taken on the name Albert Abraham during immigration and people called him Al now. He started working odd jobs soon after our arrival, while I took care of Pipsi and we began figuring out how to work in our professions again. I had studied a little English in Munich, but I was very shy to speak it. I wanted to speak it correctly or not at all. And I didn't like how Americans pronounced my name: they called me

"Asia" like the continent. So one day, when I saw a display of name tags in a store, I decided that Alice was the closest and nicest substitute for Asya. Edith, Mrs. Steiman, and I started going to evening school to learn English. Our life was changing quickly and could have been so happy, if not for poor Pipsi.

Instead of recovering from the journey, he seemed to get sicker every day. Since Mother knew doctors at Kew Gardens Hospital, we took Pipsi to the pediatrician there. The doctor said Pipsi had pneumonia and admitted him right away.

Mother and Edith spent the night with me at the hospital. At some point, the nurses told me to go to the waiting room and take a nap.

"Yes, lie down a little bit," Mother said. "We'll stay with him."

I was in a daze, didn't really know what was going on, so I listened to them. Next thing I remember is them calling me in and seeing my little boy, lifeless. He looked like he was asleep. I could never talk about this, and even writing about it now is very difficult. Today these babies are called blue babies, and they are operated on and often they live.

We had a funeral and little Nathan Genis was buried in the cemetery in Queens. The pain was indescribable. Al leaned against me and cried. I couldn't even cry. Most of Mother's family came, which was some comfort. One cousin said, "You should have another baby right away." But we couldn't afford it. In the same way Al never wanted to talk about his past, he didn't want to talk about losing our son, but I know it was very hard for him. I too suppressed my grief and got a job soon after my baby's funeral. Somehow we just went on.

Not much later, our extended family experienced the next terrible loss. Aunt Celia, Father's youngest sister whose husband, Velvel, had died in Föhrenwald, had been sent to Cleveland by her sponsors, together with her daughters, Sorahle and Miriam. Because Celia was a single mother and needed to work, she had to put her girls into an orphanage for the time being. Soraleh was the baby who was born in the bunker in Golducha. From when she was tiny, she had a sunny and bright disposition and put a smile on everybody's face. Now, at the age of nine, she contracted hepatitis and died. Edith and Al went to the funeral. I don't remember why I didn't go. Maybe my family was afraid that seeing Celia burying her child would be too much for me such a short time after my own child's death.

Alice Singer-Genis with Emunah Herzog

At evening school, I met a woman who worked in a cosmetic factory, Helena Rubinstein. The way this woman described the work made it sound glamorous but, in reality, it was hard labor. They put me on the conveyor belt. The conveyor belt moved quickly, and every woman had a function. I had to close the bottles. I got dizzy just looking at the belt with all the little bottles moving so fast. After three months, I got sick, missed a few days work, and got fired.

By this time, Al had steady employment in a grocery store, in the dairy department, and got me a job in the store as well. But I had to work in the freezer in the backroom and wrap meat. It was so cold in there! I did what I had to do and worked there for quite a while, until they transferred me to another store, which was too far for me to travel.

Then I briefly worked in a dentist's office as a dental assistant and receptionist. He liked my assisting and especially how clean I kept the instruments and how I sterilized them. But he said my English was not good enough to answer the phone, and I lost my job once again.

One day, I had to go to the hospital for some blood work. The lab technician was a Belarusian named Victor. Before the war, Victor lived in Vilno and was a teacher.

"One of our lab technicians is pregnant and will leave soon," he told me when he realized my situation. His face was secretive. "The boss isn't aware of it yet. I'll let you know the right time to apply."

Victor kept his promise, and that's how I finally found decent employment. He also trained me. Fortunately my medical background helped and I learned fast.

From the first day in New York, we tried to find out how to practice dentistry, how to work in our profession. We knocked on every door, but every door seemed to be closed to us. I even went to New Jersey, to a medical center. The man in charge who hired dentists interviewed me for a long time. Once he found out I had a husband, he lost interest. The only possibility was to go to NYU Dental School for three more years, getting credit for the first year only. But first one needed an interview, which was hard to get.

We soon realized that it was not feasible for both of us go to dental school. Aside from the fact that they didn't accept husband and wife in the same class, it was financially impossible; tuition was very high. So we decided that Al would apply. In the meantime he got a job through a friend in a jewelry store. Al worked very hard for a year and a half and was finally accepted to NYU Dental School. A friend of ours, Lucille, was instrumental in getting Al the interview. The way it worked was that the places of students who dropped out after the first year were filled with European students. It would likely have been easier for me to get in, because few women attended dental school. But, in those days, choosing me to pursue my career over Al pursuing his was not even a topic of discussion.

It was difficult for our students. For the next three years Al went to NYU every day while I worked in the medical laboratory at Queens General Hospital. In the evening, Al studied with a friend he met in school, a Ukrainian dentist, Dr. Kinrad. I worked from nine to five, sometimes longer, and, when I came home, I cooked dinner for the guys and me.

New York in the fifties was a city of many ethnic neighborhoods. To me, it looked like a multitude of small towns put together into one large city. Each neighborhood had a different flavor with its own restaurants and its own language. Our budget was tight but, because we were frugal, we could afford to sample a variety of foods, each in its unique atmosphere. I fondly remember eating Hungarian and German food for reasonable prices. It was then that we discovered Chinese food, which I've loved ever since the very first bite. We also got together with old friends in our free time and, occasionally, we treated ourselves to a movie. Mother's relatives visited us often in the beginning. Later Al was very busy with school and didn't have time to socialize, but we always kept in touch with our family.

When Mother and Edith had first arrived, they had stayed in Brooklyn with Aunt Mina and Uncle Jack. Mina was Mother's sister. They lived in a two-family-house and had a son and two daughters. Aunt Mina and her husband lived downstairs. Her daughter Shirley with her family lived upstairs. Mother had a sister, Rose, who also lived in Brooklyn. She was a seamstress and worked hard. Rose had two sons and a husband who was very handsome. Both of her sons were in the military during the war. Mother's older brother died. He left a wife and two sons. They were also both in the military service during the war. Irvin was a teacher and Manuel was a lawyer. Manuel's wife was Bea. Irvin had been stationed in Germany and he had married a German who converted.

Cousin Nina was a very pleasant woman. Mother's other brother, Sam, lived in Syracuse, NY. Uncle Sam and Aunt Anna's modest home was warm and full of love for everybody. They had three sons who served in the service. Cousin Bernie told me that Grandfather Wolf Smith, Mother's father, used to stay with them and was buried in the cemetery in Syracuse, as was grandmother. I was grateful to have a large extended family, but we didn't have as much in common as with my family back home where we survived together. I missed them. However, the wonders of America took over.

I Won't Die Hungry

Al and I in New York.
(Circa 1955)

The first year in New York, we went to celebrate New Year's at Time Square. This custom continues and it's bigger than ever. We never went again, but I've watched it on television every year unless we were at a house party. It was exciting to walk with thousands of people for Al,

Edith, and me. It was one experience I will never forget. Another exciting experience was to see Judy Garland perform at the Madison Square Garden. We also went on a boat trip for new Americans. On the boat were young people from various countries. Many brought accordions, guitars, and other musical instruments. People were singing in their native languages. The outing was arranged by an organization for new Americans. It was much fun. Life for new immigrants was not easy, so every event was a special bonus. Sometimes, on Sundays, Edith and I went for a milkshake or an ice cream sundae. I liked a strawberry sundae best. We also liked to go shopping together and find clothes on sale. It was possible to look decent and even stylish on a budget, which was one of the wonders of America and I appreciated it. A very special occasion was to see South Pacific on Broadway. It was the first American musical I saw, quite different from the operettas I saw in Munich. I loved South Pacific.

While Al made friends in dental school, I made friends in the hospital. Queens General was a University Hospital, so there were interns and residents as well as students who studied medicine in Europe and came for the summer to the States to practice at Queens General. There was also a nursing school. Many people who worked in the laboratory came from Europe and were intelligent people: Victor, as I said, was a teacher from Belarus; Anthony was a pharmacist in Lithuania; his wife was a physician; and there was a Russian woman called Schlapnikova. She was married to a doctor and she was very funny and made us laugh. She spoke terrible broken English, but she didn't care. I was fond of a Hungarian lady who had been a violinist and now also worked as a lab technician. Our boss was woman physician from Hungary.

I took the bus to and from work. One evening, while I waited for the bus, it was getting dark and started to rain, so I stepped into the booth. The bus stop was right in front of the hospital. There was a man in the booth, and he started a conversation. He was Italian, a resident physician in urology at Queens General. He got on the same bus and sat down next to me. We had a lot in common. He had studied in Italy with a friend of mine from Vilno. Before long, David started coming to the lab to visit. Somehow he always managed to meet me during the lunch break. Often he waited until I finished my work and took me home. He was handsome, intelligent, and European.

I Won't Die Hungry

One day, he asked me out for pizza. It was the first time I tasted pizza. He was fascinated and listened intently when I told him about the partisans. Another time he asked me to go out for borsht and he liked it very much. I invited him to my house and he came and met Mother and Al. By this time, Edith was already married and had moved to Chicago.

David had told me that he was dating a nurse. She was the nurse in charge on his floor and he took her out sometimes. But then he told me that he didn't care for her. I asked him how she felt about him. He said she knew that he was not serious about her but wanted to go out with him anyhow. Then one day, David asked me and Al to go with him to the beach. The nurse was in the car and we went to Jones Beach. It was a beautiful day but I didn't feel good. My conscience, my so-called superego, bothered me. I was not sophisticated like he was. Another time, when he dropped in to see me like he often did, Al came to pick me up. The men were civil to each other, but I felt uncomfortable. As time went on my discomfort increased. Victor didn't want David to come to the lab and the two started to fight. I experienced many new feelings from anger to jealousy to guilt to disappointment and was not happy anymore. Finally David finished his residency and moved to California. I never heard from him again.

When Al was in his last year of dental school I became pregnant. It was summer and the heat was stifling. I was in the sixth week of pregnancy and went in a jeep with a driver to take blood from patients who were homebound. The lab technicians took turns and I had to do it once a month. Ordinarily, I enjoyed it, but this time I was very tired. Soon after this, it was my turn to come early for the diabetic clinic, before the laboratory opened. Diabetic patients lined up and I had to test their urine before the nurse and the doctor came. I fainted right there. The patients called for help. A nurse soon arrived and I was taken upstairs and examined internally against my wish. I still remember the nurse, she looked like an old maid to me.

"It is the law," she said with a stern face when I told her I had a private doctor who told me not to be examined until three months of pregnancy.

The resident who examined me was not experienced and it was painful, but I tried to be disciplined and didn't complain. After this, I was bleeding and stayed home, in bed. A few days later the bleeding got worse. Mother, who worked in Kew Gardens Hospital on the obstetric ward, knew several gynecology doctors. She had picked the best doctor for me and I had met him before the bleeding occurred. He was a refugee from Germany. I was hospitalized, and this doctor took good care of me, but I still lost my baby. It was a very painful experience, physically as well as emotionally. The doctor was compassionate and understanding and had a good relationship with his patients. This characteristic made Al so well-liked by his patients later when he practiced dentistry. Having Mother with me was a great support. The doctor recommended that I wait three months to get pregnant again. I waited three months and became pregnant.

This time, I was careful and the pregnancy went well. I watched what I ate, and I rested and took long walks. Two wonderful things happened to us in July of 1956: The birth of our baby and the graduation of Al from dental school. Finally, he could practice dentistry.

The graduation was in the Bronx. He actually received an award from NYU at the 100th anniversary of the dental school. It was an extremely hot day in July; I believe it was a Friday. Very pregnant, I made it to the graduation and then, over the weekend, I went into labor. Al and Mother took me to Kew Gardens Hospital where our daughter, Naomi, was born.

When I came home with our new baby, Mother took a week of vacation from the hospital. She stayed with me and took care of us. I was very lucky to have my mother. Today I appreciate it more than ever. Nobody can help like your mother, especially when she is a registered nurse and a midwife.

After graduation from dental school, Al volunteered to serve in the Army for two years. He was sent to Texas for six weeks of basic training. He left a week after Naomi was born. I lived with Mother like before. She went back to work, but still was very helpful to me. I took a leave of absence for a year from the hospital. Naomi was such a good baby and I very much enjoyed taking care of her. I took her for a walk every day and loved to play with her. She was beautiful and had big blue eyes. I called her my blue-eyed angel.

Somehow the six weeks went by and Al came back. He told me that he would be stationed in Fort Monmouth, New Jersey. After five years in New York, we moved to New Jersey. Another chapter in our lives began.

Chapter Eleven

AL WAS STATIONED AT FORT Monmouth in 1956. I was thirty years old. We went to look for a place to live and decided to move to a military community in Eatontown which was close to the base. We moved to a block of two-story apartments. Our apartment was on a corner, so we had more privacy. A lawyer and his family lived next door, the first Southerners we got to know. He was also an officer. The military families were guarded by the MP. We had two bedrooms and a bathroom upstairs, the living room and kitchen were downstairs. Mother had to make a choice whether to stay in New York or to move with us. It was a difficult decision for her to leave her apartment and job, but she decided to come along. We took her furniture from the apartment in New York with us which made us feel at home in our new quarters immediately. I still remember that we bought a dryer with Al's first paycheck.

The two years in Fort Monmouth were among the best years of my life. Al worked in the Army dental clinic. Finally he could work in his profession and he liked it. He learned a lot in the clinic. The first year he was a lieutenant, the second year a captain. We were with a group of young dentists and physicians from different places all over America. Some were married, others were single, and all were friendly and cheerful, trying to make the best of the situation. Many were in for two years like us. Everybody was in the same boat. This was a good thing about the Army; unlike civilians who compete with each other, it was relaxing. The social life was fabulous. We went to the officers club for various occasions. The dental corps had its table, so did the medical corps, etc. Colonel O'Grady kept the dental group together. It was so much fun to go to different celebrations. I had a feeling of belonging. It was festive and traditional. There were countless activities for women such as luncheons and other functions. They had a list of babysitters and Mother helped also, so that I could leave Naomi and attend. Al and I were popular and we made numerous friends. We were invited to many parties and we enjoyed it. English was the only spoken language. I spoke English constantly and it improved considerably. In New York, I had spoken Polish, German, Russian, and Yiddish, but here I spoke only English. It even became the language we spoke at home.

After about a year in Fort Monmouth, we were able to buy a piano. What a delight that was. I bought it for a reasonable price from an old Italian man who built pianos out of used parts. This one he had assembled from a grand piano and it had a beautiful sound. The only problem was that the keyboard missed keys on both sides, which interfered with playing most classical pieces properly. But I made the best of it. Our neighbor, the Southern gentleman, gave me a book of piano music that I still have today.

In 1957, Edith gave birth to her first child, Helene Joy. It truly was a joy for all of us, especially Mother. And we became American citizens that year, which was a big celebration. Captain Parker, a dentist, and Lieutenant Reynolds, a nurse, were our witnesses. We were happy and excited and elated. To be a wife of an American officer was a big honor and it made me proud.

The New Year celebration at the officer's club was an affair to remember. The women wore gowns. The men looked handsome in uniforms. The club was beautifully decorated. It was an elegant ball with entertainment and dancing. Fortunately I recuperated from a bad cold and could go to the ball.

For a while I seemed to get one cold after the other, but then we got some good news: I was pregnant again. We were so excited with this wonderful news!

And yet another happy event was Mother's remarriage. She married a man she knew from way back in Vilno, Philip Galerkin. The marriage ceremony was performed in Brooklyn at Aunt Mina's home, Mother's sister.

Cousin Mira and her husband, Simon, visited us in Fort Monmouth. They had lived in Pittsburgh for a couple of years; Simon was part of a research team for a new diabetes medication.

Time was marching on and before we knew it, the two years were nearly over. We had to think about what to do next, where to go. The colonel wanted us to stay in the Army for good, for Al to become a career officer for twenty years. This was tempting. We thought about it at great length. It would have been a secure life with many privileges. It involved moving from base to base, which sounded exciting.

But after a long deliberation and numerous discussions we decided to do it the hard way for the children's sake. We thought the children would be better off to live in a community rather than to travel from place to place. So our search for a dental office started.

Unlike the other dentists, who could return home, we had no place to go. Al met with a man who was locating dentists. We traveled far and wide in New York State, looking for a place to work and live. By now I was very pregnant again. Often we took Naomi with us. She was only two years old and a good traveler. I wanted to live close to Mother who had moved back to New York when she got married. But Al, still a country boy at heart, didn't want to live in the city. And we had no money to start our new life with. A friend of ours in the Army, Elmar LaCasale, used to say, "Poor Al has no place to go. His wife is pregnant, he has a two-year-old, and no money."

I was sad and troubled to leave Fort Monmouth. I had a good obstetrician in Red Bank, NJ, close to Eatontown where we lived, and I had hoped to deliver the baby there. We had heard that sometimes people were allowed to stay a little longer in the military housing. But, unfortunately, as soon as Al was not in the Army anymore, which was two weeks before my expected delivery date, we had to clear our quarters.

So the search for a place to work and live continued. We looked at many offices in the New York area. Al's Ukrainian friend, Dr. Kinrad, who Al studied with while going to NYU Dental School, had moved to Rochester, NY. Dr. Kinrad never went to the Army; he opened his dental office in Rochester and was doing well. He contacted Al about a dental office in Rochester for sale. Al wrote to the dentist and they agreed for us to come upstate, to meet and to see the office.

Al, Naomi, and I got in the car again. We stopped in Syracuse, NY, to visit Uncle Sam, slept at his house, and drove in the morning to Rochester which is close to Syracuse. First we visited Dr. Kinrad and his family. Naomi played with their big German shepherd. The dog was much bigger than she was, but she was not afraid at all. Then we went together to see the office. It was in a working class neighborhood. The dentist was pleased that Naomi and I came along. The meeting went well, although there were some things that Al and the other dentist didn't agree on. For example, we were expected to move into the apartment above the dental office, something Al was completely against. The other dentist had his brother-in-law, a business man, negotiate for him. I remember this man at one point saying: "You are two stubborn dentists." But when we left the office, Al and Dr. Kinrad agreed that this had a lot of potential. We seriously considered moving to Rochester and spent the rest of the day exploring Rochester, which is an attractive, cultured city with a good university.

In the evening we went back to Syracuse to sleep at Uncle Sam's house. I put Naomi to bed and soon we went to lie down as well. But I couldn't go to sleep and found myself quietly crying into my pillow.

Al noticed it. "Why are you crying?" he asked.

"I want to be close to my mother," I answered and, as soon as the words came out of my mouth, the tears really started flowing. So we decided not to move to Rochester, but started looking in the greater New York area.

After some more searching, an office in Peekskill became available. Peekskill is an hour away from New York, close enough to Mother, so Al went to look at it. It wasn't much, but it was a beginning. The price was affordable, and we were running out of time. After brief deliberations, Al signed the deal. By now I couldn't travel anymore, was ready to deliver any day, so I stayed at Mother's apartment with Naomi while Mother went with Al to find an apartment in Peekskill for us. Little did I know then of the ups and downs this small, unassuming town had in store for me.

Chapter Twelve

FINDING AN APARTMENT IN PEEKSKILL in 1958 was easier said than done, but eventually Mother and Al found us a place to live in a two-family house, above a family with five children. The youngest was Naomi's age. We thought it would be good for Naomi to have a playmate, but it didn't work out that way. The little girl was a hyperactive child who lived on sedatives and other drugs and didn't know how to play with other children.

As soon as we moved to Peekskill, Al devoted himself to his office and I had to face long days and evenings with Naomi by myself. Two weeks later, on September 24, I gave birth to Bobby in the old Peekskill Hospital. We now have a new hospital, the Hudson Valley Hospital Center, which is excellent, but the old hospital was far behind the times. I saw the obstetrician only once in his office and then I never saw him in the delivery room, because they sedated me before he arrived. He was the only obstetrician in town and was very busy. I still know his wife and only recently saw her in the beauty parlor.

When I came home, I didn't feel well. I don't know what happened. Maybe the hardship of the last months took its toll, and I didn't have my mother to take care of me. Al hired a baby nurse from the agency. She was old and treated Naomi harshly. I was sick in bed, Al was away in his office, and Naomi had to adjust to a little stranger in the house. It was difficult for her and for me.

The circumcision, the Bris, took place in our apartment. It was a lovely party, catered by the Jewish delicatessen in town. For me, it was difficult to accept the ritual and ceremony. An old-fashioned Moel who circumcised every Jewish boy in town did the circumcision. He was very respected in Peekskill. It was a trauma for me.

I've studied the subject since, tried to understand the reasoning behind it, yet even now, I always feel sorry for the baby who is innocent and doesn't know what's being done to him and why. In retrospect, I think it wasn't so much the deed itself, but it was the next day when the Moel came back, how he didn't wash his hands and squeezed the little penis. My baby boy cried terribly and I almost fainted. This made me furious and question the whole ritual.

Al and I had joined the First Hebrew Congregation, and soon after Bobby was born, I enrolled Naomi at their nursery school. It was just being organized. The mothers participated, and the teacher was a kind woman. It was enjoyable for Naomi to play with other children and I had more time for the baby.

The nursery school was something to be proud of. Now it is much bigger than it was at that time and still very popular, except now all children are accepted, then it was just a Jewish center. I was on the nursery school board and enjoyed that responsibility but, generally, I didn't like to go to meetings with the local women. I felt like a stranger. I didn't have much in common with them; I was a professional woman with entirely different interests. And, even though I didn't feel like talking about my experiences in Europe, I felt that the American Jews were different from us who had survived.

I missed Fort Monmouth very much; I missed the commissary, the officer's club, the swimming pool, and the beach. Most of all, I missed the comradery. My nights weren't lonely there, whereas now Al continued to work late, and the evenings by myself – especially once I had put the children to bed – were extremely difficult for me.

After renting the apartment for one year, we wanted to escape the noise from downstairs and we started looking for a house. We searched for a ranch house without stairs at an affordable price, and we found such a house in the town of Cortlandt. The schools were better there. There were children to play with and it was a good area for the children to grow up. The house was simple but comfortable, surrounded by sturdy oaks and maple trees in the back and delicate birches in the front. We bought the property on Birchwood Lane in 1959 and I am writing these words there in 2009, fifty years later. Over the years we added on to the house and always took good care of it. It always was and still is a very well-built house.

I enjoyed my children and my house, found much pleasure in gardening, and admired the surrounding countryside. Yet underneath it all I remained unhappy. Sometimes we took a drive into the country on Sundays with the children.

The Hudson Valley is very beautiful. No wonder that artists came here to paint and establish the so-called Hudson Valley Art School. The area is especially spectacular in October when the leaves change color and turn from green to many magnificent shades of yellow and orange and deep red. Only a few minutes' drive from our house are breathtaking views, like the one looking down at the river from Bear Mountain. The mountains surrounding the majestic Hudson are always green. They are sloped mildly and delicately, unlike the Alps which are much steeper and tall. Many antique stores attract people from the city. The view out of our big living room window overlooking our porch and big back yard is like a painting, no matter what season, even in the winter when the sun causes the snow to sparkle like diamonds. Unfortunately, I was often stuck in the house when it snowed and the roads were slippery and sometimes closed. At 4:00 p.m., it got dark and the evenings were even more excruciatingly long and lonely.

Until we moved to Peekskill, I always pursued a goal; if it wasn't my own career, it was to help Al finish dental school, and later to find an office and a place to live. Suddenly, I didn't feel needed and useful anymore. I kept mulling over how hard I had worked and how many sacrifices I had made to have a career, and what a terrible thing it was to waste a mind. How I had wanted to be a doctor! And now that I was a dentist, I couldn't even work in my profession. In retrospect, I think it was during those endlessly lonesome evenings when I first began feeling angry. Angry at Cousin Mira and Al for persuading me to let go of my dream of becoming a physician and to switch to dentistry instead. Angry at society for holding me down and condemning me to be a housewife. And most of all, angry at myself for letting it all happen. Without being aware of it, I turned my anger inward and it slowly began manifesting as depression. To my defense, I must say that I was conditioned to recognize my husband as the primary breadwinner, and I never wanted it any other way.

I had always hoped that as soon as we were able to afford it, I would go back to dental school. But it meant attending school for three more years. I would have had to live in New York and come home on the weekends. Who would take care of my children? After much thinking and soul searching, I decided to stay home and take care of the children. It seems like such a good decision today, but at the time it was easier said than done.

I was not happy with my life. I hated being a "Hausfrau", a suburban housewife, in Peekskill. The small town bored me beyond words. The relationship between men and women was very different than I was accustomed to. At parties or dinners, the women socialized with other women and men with other men. In the beginning, when we came to Peekskill, the men paid more attention to me and I felt that it caused some of the women to resent me. I was not used to the games they played. They made me nervous.

And this wasn't the only cultural alienation I was up against. I remember the following event as if it was yesterday, even though it took place fifty years ago, not long after we moved into our house on Birchwood Lane.

Al and I had invited a few neighbors over for a buffet dinner. I'd prepared cold foods – roast beef, vegetables, salads, that sort of thing. A few days earlier I had bought an electric knife, and this was the first time we used it. I still have it today, and it still works.

For some reason, I remembered the incident from the woods, when we were surrounded and shot at by the Germans, and when Mother asked me how I could eat in such a situation and I said, "At least I won't be hungry when I die." I told this story to our guests, thinking of it as funny.

"We don't want to hear about this," a woman said with a stern face.

Heat shot into my face, and my heart pounded fast in my ribcage all the way into my throat. I felt both stupid and embarrassed, wanting to explain that I had only meant to relate the humor of the situation, but my mouth was frozen shut. I had rarely felt like talking about what happened to us with our American friends, despite most of them being Jewish, but this sealed my lips about our past for a long time to come.

What helped somewhat was that we had family in Yorktown and in Peekskill. The Flowers, Pauline and Jack, as well as Mother's cousin,

Irvin London, and his wife, Fay, were nice to us. It gave me a feeling of family. I spoke to Mother almost every day on the phone and stayed in close touch with Edith who'd given birth to her second daughter, Nancy. But in the synagogue I felt like an orphan. Most Peekskill Jews were Americans whose parents or grandparents had originally come from Russia, Poland, Lithuania, and Hungary. Most were professionals, business people, even politicians. Yet on holidays and special occasions, I thought about my family members who were killed and then I felt lonely. At Bar Mitzvahs and graduations, I felt bad for my children who didn't have many relatives.

A few children lived in our neighborhood who went to the same nursery school as Naomi and we became part of a carpool. The first year was difficult. Al was off on Wednesdays and the women wanted me to drive on Wednesdays, but Al took a course at the Medical Center in Valhalla and I did not have the car. Every Tuesday, I went through hell trying to find somebody to drive the carpool. It was extremely unpleasant. A year later, we bought a small rambler so I had my own car and could drive the children.

Al's dental practice flourished. He was devoted to his patients, very busy, and extremely well-liked. His patients and his staff were the most important part of his life. I wanted to work with him in the office, even just part-time, but he wouldn't hear of it.

"You are a dentist and to work as a clerk will make you unhappy," he said.

And he didn't talk with me about what went on in the office. I felt excluded and not needed anymore, which did not have a positive effect on our marriage. Today I see some of what happened differently. For one thing, I think Al wanted to be the boss in his own territory and did not want me to interfere. Al wanted to keep his professional and personal lives separate, and was also concerned that because of my health problems, working and being involved in his office would be too much for me. Before, when we lived in Munich, I was the one who attended and graduated from dental school first, it was my idea for him to become a dentist and, even in New York, my input had great importance as I worked to support us while he went to school. Somehow, he needed to show his independence now. I also realize that Al's behavior was his way of coping with the trauma, the tremendous losses and pain we went through during the war. Just like he never wanted to talk about his experiences as a partisan, he closed down part of himself. Unfortunately in the process he shut me out for many years as well.

At the time, none of it made sense to me and I was despondent. I couldn't understand why now that I had wonderful children, a successful husband, and a beautiful house, now that I could afford to buy fine clothes and many of the so-called good things in life, I felt more miserable than during most of the hardships in Europe. Despite increasing my involvement in Hadassah and volunteering in the Hospital Auxiliary, life didn't seem to improve for me for a couple of years. Nothing satisfied my hunger for feeling stimulated, useful, and appreciated. So I decided to try to go back to school while the children were still small after all. But things got worse before they got better.

I went to NYU in New York, once a week, to a class for foreign students to learn English. I slept over at Mother's. It was winter, and I remember how I started feeling weaker and weaker. I was losing strength in my legs and arms. Mother took me to her doctor who immediately sent me to the NYU hospital.

By the time I came to the hospital, I could not walk anymore; they had to transport me in a wheelchair. I went through many tests, some of them quite painful. Yet I was getting worse and worse, was getting stiff like a board. Mother and my stepfather visited me every evening. At the end I could not talk anymore and could hardly breathe. I was an enigma to the doctors. They expected the worst and didn't know what it was. Finally a resident from South America took my medical history again. It had been taken hundreds of times before. He found out that in Munich I had a hyperthyroid gland condition, which was cured by medication. This led him to test my potassium and they found that the potassium was very, very low. I still don't understand why they didn't notice that before. They started to give me potassium. Slowly, very slowly, the movement in my fingers and then in my arms and in my legs returned. It took a week for my body to be able to move again. I was in the hospital for three weeks. The question was how did I lose my potassium? They had different theories, but they suspected that the reason was my kidneys. Nephrology, the kidney specialty, was in its infancy; it just started to develop as a specialty. Up to that time it was considered part of internal medicine.

I Won't Die Hungry

In the meantime, my small children were at home with Al. They went to school by bus. They were home alone until he came back from work. He got them so-called TV dinners – prepared food in a box – for dinner. Nothing like my home cooked meals. Naomi spoke with me on the phone, which raised my spirits. She was always cheerful. This is her personality. But Bobby didn't speak with me. He was very young and probably thought that I abandoned him.

Interestingly enough, while I was in the hospital, the thoughts about wanting a career vanished completely. All my mental energy was focused on staying alive and being able to take care of my children again. The happy day I returned will always stay in my memory. When Bobby came from school and saw me at home, his eyes showed happiness that I will never forget.

I had to take potassium every day but, after I while, I had a relapse and started getting paralyzed again. I called my internist and told him about my experience in the hospital in New York. He ordered me to take six tablespoons of potassium and go to the hospital immediately. I was given more potassium in the hospital and, after a few days, I was better and was discharged home with orders for more potassium. Sometime later, my internist told me about the Department for Nephrology in the Grasslands Hospital in Valhalla in Westchester. Today it is the Westchester Medical Center. Kidney transplants and open heart surgery are being performed there. The doctor in charge ordered a biopsy of the kidneys.

I checked into the hospital myself. A friend of mine, a woman I knew from Munich, was taking an internship in dentistry in the hospital and stopped in to see me in the evening. I shared the room with a physician, who had been in a car accident and was hospitalized and on bed rest. The next morning, I was scheduled for the biopsy in the operating room. I didn't eat or drink before I went to bed. I believe I was given some medication. At night I had to go to the bathroom. I got up, walked around the other bed, and just before I reached the bathroom, I got dizzy and fainted. As I fell, I lost consciousness and hit my face against the open door. The patient in the next bed heard me falling and started yelling for help. For some reason, we didn't have call bells, but she yelled so loud that soon somebody came and found me in a pool of blood on the floor. I was still unconscious when they took me to the operating room. I had sustained a severe cut on my nose, and a resident from South America stitched it up. The next morning I was taken to the operating room again for the biopsy. Al came to see me afterwards. I looked awful. My face was terribly swollen, all black and blue. It took a long time for my face to heal, but I did not have cosmetic surgery. A small scar remained for the rest of my life and I am used to it now. At the time, I had to face bigger problems.

The kidney biopsy showed that I lost 75% of my kidney function. It meant I had to function on 25% of my kidney. They put me on a small amount of antibiotics to prevent infections. I also had to take potassium every day, which continued to be low. The nephrologist told me to live a normal life, and I did. Not much later, the opportunity arose for me to join a Zionist Organization on a trip to Israel. Mother offered to stay with Al and the children, and off I went.

Naomi and Bob in our house.
Peekskill, New York (Early 1960's)

Chapter Thirteen

My first visit to Israel remains in my memory as one of the highlights of my life.

On the way, we stopped in Rome for three days. As soon as I set foot on European soil, some of the heaviness I had felt for years lifted.

I had never been to Italy before, and the beauty of Rome overwhelmed me. We visited the Vatican, St. Peter's Cathedral, the Sistine Chapel; we explored the Coliseum and walked the Spanish Steps; we saw the Old Synagogue, one of the oldest known Jewish houses of prayer in Europe. The monuments of Rome and its fountains are unforgettable. We even had a chance to see the Rome of today with its bustling streets and busy traffic and we went to a nightclub. In three days I had a good overview of Rome. I still think it is one of the most beautiful cities in the world. In the years to come, I had opportunity to see it even better, but the first impression was the strongest and has remained with me forever.

I'll never forget the moment when I got off the plane in Tel Aviv and saw my family standing there like one person, waiting for me. There were so many of the people I lived with in the woods: Aunt Hannah and Uncle Moshe, Aunt Ella, Cousin Asya, and Cousin Aryeh! There was Aunt Brocha, Mother's oldest sister, whom I hadn't seen since I was a child. And there was Cousin Mira, who had lived with us in the Singer House; we still looked alike and felt more like sisters than cousins. Even now, as I'm writing this, I am overcome with emotion. I just broke down crying, yet these were the happiest tears I ever shed. All the emotions which I had held inside let loose, and I felt light and easy. I loved everybody under the sun. I had been so lonely and unhappy. Seeing my family made me feel like I could breathe again. From that moment on, this journey became like a pilgrimage to me.

I traveled with the group and got to see the country. In the sixties, not too many people ventured to Israel. Mostly Zionists and people who wanted to visit their family. Mira asked the tour guide for permission to come with us to the next town to sleep over at the hotel. This way we could spend another day together. It was such a joy to sit in the tour bus with Mira.

I fell in love with every Israeli including our tour guide, who did an excellent job. Israel felt like a young country in an old land to me. It was amazing how so many nationalities lived together in such a small country, because even though they were all Jewish, they came from different countries and cultures and spoke different languages. However, everybody tried to speak Hebrew. The children spoke it naturally, and the Israelis born in Israel, the so-called Sabras, spoke it proudly. A Sabra is an Israeli native fruit that is tough on the outside but sweet on the inside.

Our guide was a Sabra. He was a handsome man with blue eyes and dark blond hair of medium height. He spoke English, which he had learned while he was in the Haganah[7], with a British accent. Like all Israelis, he was proud of his country and it was obvious that he liked showing it to us; he did it with pride and love. We were of the same generation and found a lot to talk about. Somehow he looked both familiar and different. European and American men wore ties. Like other Israeli men, he didn't wear a tie. It was an informal look, an unusual look in those days to me.

We traveled all over Israel and I visited family and friends in many different places. It was the late spring, and the weather was warm and sunny wherever we went. In Tel Aviv, I visited Cousin Aryeh and his wife, Rina. They had two sons and a daughter and I got there just in time for one of the boys' fourth birthday party. It was a lovely children's party with puppets and balloons. Israelis lived in apartments, not in homes, but they were happy. Aryeh was a colonel in the army, and an engineer. He still loved to talk about Bomka the famous partisan.

In Haifa, we went to the Baha'i Temple on top of the mountain. I felt

---

[7] A Jewish paramilitary organization in what was then Palestine which later became the core of the Israel Defense Forces

that Adam and Eve's paradise must have looked like this beautiful garden with its magnificent flowers and exotic trees. In Hadera, I visited Aunt Ella and Asya, and Aunt Brocha and her family. Asya was married – her husband's name was Aryeh, too – and they had two daughters. Aunt Brocha's son was a real "Chalutz" – a pioneer. He had come to Palestine even before his parents, had lived in a kibbutz as a young boy. Now he was married and had a son and daughter. I don't remember the name of the place where Aunt Hannah and Uncle Moshe lived. I think Uncle Moshe never really felt at home in Israel, always missed his land and the nursery in Gleboki. He had aged considerably since I last saw him. But Aunt Hannah was energetic and kept a marvelous vegetable garden. I was told that she was the first one in the development to plant a garden. Uncle Moshe had said to her, "Nothing will grow in this sand." But she did it anyway, and before long it bloomed. When the neighbors saw her success, they followed her example. Aunt Hannah still loved to cook and could still make a chicken stretch to feed many mouths at her table.

We got to see the Independence Day Parade. Somehow the tour guide managed to reserve especially good seats for our group. It was a very happy event. The people from New York I traveled with couldn't get over the little girls carrying big guns and marching like men. We also went to the Galilee, to the Dead Sea, and of course to Jerusalem. We planted trees like most tourists do and did other touristy things, but I didn't feel like a tourist. I felt at home.

The city of Jerusalem was still divided between Israel and Jordan. We stayed in the Israeli part. To me, Jerusalem seemed in league with ancient cities like Rome and Athens, yet it had a beauty of its own. It is built from white stone and, when the sun shines, it looks like gold. It was small at that time but very distinguished. We saw all the holy and historic places, visited a mosque, and went to a philharmonic concert. Al's Aunt Liba had moved to Jerusalem from Sweden. We met in a hotel for lunch. She looked elegant, wore a coat with small minks around the collar and a smart little hat. But she ate like she hadn't eaten in a long time and seemed lonely. I gave her some money and she was very grateful. Later, Mira took care of her. Sadly, toward the end of her life, Aunt Liba became senile and constantly lamented that everybody was stealing her antiques. Mira and her husband, Simon, had a lovely apartment in Jerusalem. Mira worked as a nurse and Simon was a doctor in Hadassah

Hospital. They didn't have children. Their apartment was furnished modern in a very nice, quiet taste.

I briefly thought about how much Mira had influenced my life, like switching from medicine to dentistry, and immigrating to America instead of Israel. When I visited my friends from Munich – and there were many I had stayed in touch with – I noticed that everyone was doing well. The dentists were in private practice and some were teaching in dental school. Physicians and engineers worked in hospitals and in other good positions. A whole group of us got together at a country club in Savion, a prestigious neighborhood not far from Tel Aviv. While many of the Israelis struggled to make ends meet, my friends all seemed to be doing well. I remember a friend of mine – she had always been ambitious and was a cardiologist now – said to me, "I don't like America. They can turn a bright girl like you into a housewife." But I don't remember dwelling on any regrets. I was overjoyed to see everyone doing well and marveled at the reality of the Jewish State which was but a distant dream when I was a youngster.

When we went to Yad Vashem, the memorial museum to six million Holocaust victims, I found every town I looked for. I cried when I saw the Gleboki Ghetto and the names of my grandfather and grandmother – Irma and Sarah Chava Singer – and Uncle Mula's. And, of course, I recognized countless other names. Tears kept rolling down my face when I saw Ponary, the place outside Vilno, where over 70,000 Jews were murdered, where I lost much of my family and many friends. I thought about my cousin, Gita, who was four months younger than I. I remembered how we played together when we were children. She perished in Ponary. Visiting Yad Vashem was reliving the past for me. Our whole group left there like we were leaving a funeral.

Being in Israel brought out a myriad of feelings in me. It was a healing experience and moved me forward emotionally. I felt vulnerable but strong at the same time. I also promised myself to come back with my husband and children and not to travel alone anymore.

On the way home, we stopped for three days in Paris. I got my roommate back. She was a Hungarian woman about my age who shared the room with me in Italy, but in Israel she stayed with her mother. It was enjoyable to share the room with another woman and we got along well.

Of course, Paris is a beautiful city, but after the two weeks in Israel everything looked pale to me. We toured the city by bus and went to the usual tourist places like the Cathedral of Notre Dame, which I read about so much before, and Montmartre where many famous artists used to live. I went on my own to the Louvre and followed a group with a tour guide who was showing Leonardo da Vinci's paintings. I also met a friend who was from Vilno originally; Edith became friends with him in Lodz. Later, he stayed with us in Munich and we helped him to get into university. He graduated from the Technische Hochschule as an engineer and then moved to France. I took a taxi to meet him and got stuck in unbelievably busy traffic. It was like being in New York during rush hour. We had a lovely time in a café, reminiscing about our student days in Munich and updating each other on our lives. The next time I ventured out on my own, I took the metro, which turned out to be both comfortable and charming. It was my first time in Paris and I tried to see as much as possible. The parks and boulevards and the River Seine are so very beautiful. No wonder everybody falls in love with Paris.

When I returned home to Peekskill, my heart was full. I was so happy to take Naomi and Bobby into my arms and see their beaming little faces and to be reunited with Al. Even though I knew as much as ever that being a housewife and volunteer was not enough to satisfy me in the long run, I didn't feel as low anymore as I had before this journey.

Chapter Fourteen

AL FREQUENTLY QUOTED THE SAYING, "When you get a lemon, make lemonade." Here is an example of how he did just that:

A group of people in our neighborhood came together to discuss the possibility of building a community pool. Did we have discussions! After seemingly countless meetings, we purchased a piece of land at the end of our street. It became a wonderful community project despite many fights. We had our own lawyer, several committees, fundraising events, hired builders and carpenters, and some of us women even helped with the painting.

As soon as it was completed, Al started swimming there after work. One day, he fell in the shower and broke his arm. I believe it was the same arm that was injured when he was a partisan. A neighbor took him to the emergency room immediately, and Al was hospitalized. Right in the hospital Al hired a young dentist, Dr. Rudolph, to take care of his patients. Dr. Rudolph had been an intern at Westchester Medical Center and ended up working with Al for many years until he opened his own practice.

When Al was discharged home, he still had a cast on his arm.

"Let's go to Europe," he said, "I can't work anyway."

What a wonderful surprise!

We hired an Italian woman, Mrs. Colao, to look after the children while we were gone. Her fee was reasonable, and she had excellent recommendations and was known not to work for just anybody. When Mother heard about it, she immediately arranged to take time off from work in her husband's store. So the children had two competent and caring women looking after them.

Alice Singer-Genis with Emunah Herzog

We went with an organized group for three weeks and had the most wonderful time. Our tour started in Copenhagen, from there we traveled to Vienna, and then to Italy. We spent some time in Rome and in Sorento. It was during that trip that I saw the most beautiful spot I can ever imagine for the first time: the Amalfi Drive. Amalfi is situated high up in the mountains overlooking the Mediterranean. We stopped for coffee in a place where Jackie Kennedy had stayed. From Sorrento, we went to Capri by boat. Then we traveled to Spain and Portugal. The hotel in Mallorca was so old-world. They served an elegant dinner very late and, after each course, they changed the forks and knives and dishes.

I remember I bought pearls in Mallorca; they were not expensive at all. Almost anywhere we went I bought souvenirs for Mother and Edith and my children. An old lady in our group said, "You're always buying for your mother and sister and daughter, buy at least something for yourself." So I did. I still enjoy wearing those pearls today.

From there we went to Lisbon, where we stayed at a Ritz. It was the only time in my life that I stayed at the Ritz, and it was the grand finale of our trip. At that time, it was inexpensive to take taxis so we hired one for an hour. We asked the driver to show us the spots he thought were interesting, so he took us to a museum for coaches. Then we asked him where the locals ate, and he took us to a lunch place frequented by office people. We ordered fish. It was delicious and very, very reasonable. In those days I could eat everything and had an excellent appetite. Then we went by bus to a castle, and from there to a resort where many Americans retired.

I fondly remember this vacation along with many others. I always enjoyed traveling with Al.

In the sixties, an exodus from New York City brought scores of new physicians and a few dentists to our suburb. Al needed a bigger office. He started talking with other physicians about creating a professional medical building. Several were interested, but when it came to joining, only four were ready to make a commitment: An internist, Dr. Stevelman, who was also a cardiologist and who remained our physician for many years; Dr. Lack, an ophthalmologist; Dr. Richman, an ear, nose, and throat specialist; and Al. We bought the land in the town of Cortlandt across the street from the hospital and went through a lot of red tape. It was extremely tedious to get the permits and approvals required to build a professional building. Who had heard of such a thing before in Peekskill?

After countless meetings, we finally got permission to build a building of this kind in the area. Al was the president. The meetings continued relentlessly, often in our house, with lively discussions about how to build the structure. Each doctor had his own specifications and needs. Fortunately the four partners got along well and cooperated. We hired a Midwestern company which specialized in medical buildings. So much had to be worked out and coordinated. It was agreed it would be a two-story building with four offices on each floor. Al was a good organizer and we put a lot of time and effort into it. We called it the Community Medical Center and the opening in 1967 was a big celebration. It was announced in the local newspaper. One of the doctors' wives and I sent out invitations to professionals in the area, and of course our families and friends were invited. Mother and my stepfather came from New York City. It turned out to be a beautiful party and it really was a big breakthrough to open the first medical building in the Peekskill-Cortlandt area. The four empty offices were soon rented by other doctors.

I tried to make the best of life. Naomi and Bobby were growing up beautifully. I got more involved with Hadassah and made some women friends, and my involvement in the PTA and in the Hospital Auxiliary was enjoyable. One of the Hospital Auxiliary activities was a yearly fundraising affair called "Hospital Coffee." I participated in this activity for many years, and I still attend it at the hospital once a year. Together with a co-host, I hosted a coffee-klatch in my house and invited my neighbors from the street. This is how I met Gloria. She had moved here with her husband who was the engineer in charge of the nuclear power plant in Indian Point, which later became controversial because of its threat to the area. She took a liking to me and invited me out to lunch, and even though we were very different, we soon became good friends. She was a real Southern bell, courteous and cheerful, and much fun to be around. I enjoyed her company.

By now, Al and I had a large circle of acquaintances and friends. Many of them were newcomers from New York and other areas, and we entertained a lot. Some were Al's patients who invited us, and I would invite them back. Most of them were doctors and lawyers. Several of the women were teachers and librarians and some ran businesses. Some of the doctors' wives worked in their husbands' offices. We had beautiful parties in our house. I enjoyed the preparation and the anticipation more than anything; the actual party would go by quickly.

Al and I also joined a study group. We met in our homes and discussed subjects connected with Judaism. We studied and talked about a great many interesting books, journal articles, and sometimes discussed current events. This group lasted for a long time. Our get-togethers were exceedingly stimulating and wonderfully informal; in the beginning, we served only coffee, cake, and fruit. Later we added more food, but we deliberately kept it simple.

In the summer, I loved tending to my garden. We hired someone to help me with the heavy work, but I did much of it myself. I especially enjoyed taking care of my roses, which were exceptionally beautiful. Once or twice a year we got together with Edith's family, either at our house, at their house, or we'd travel somewhere together. To this day, we reminisce particularly fondly about a vacation in Cape Cod when Edith's third child, David, was an adorable toddler, doted on by his older sisters and cousins.

But it was not enough to satisfy me. The old nagging discontent resurfaced again and again. Ever since the medical building was completed, Al had returned to his habit of keeping me out of his professional life altogether.

When we first came to Peekskill, we found out that our old friend, Dr. Steiman – the physician who worked with Mother in Föhrenwald and who lived with his wife with Mother and Edith in New York until they found an apartment – had settled in Poughkeepsie, less than an hour from us. Dr. Steiman had been an internist in Europe, but now he practiced psychiatry. We visited each other often. He and his wife, Fania, became Al's patients. Fania was a marvelous cook and they entertained frequently. Dr. Steiman knew that I was not happy and I began consulting him. He tried to keep our marriage together in the way he knew how, but it was not always good for me. Because he understood my medical condition, he kept encouraging me not to work hard and dissuaded me from going back to school. What I didn't know until many years later was that it was Dr. Steiman who told Al not to let me work in the office.

When Pace University came to Pleasantville – about half an hour drive from our house – I went to see a guidance counselor there. She was a middle-aged woman named Mrs. Murphy, and she was married to a doctor. I told her my story.

After listening to me thoughtfully, Mrs. Murphy simply asked, "So what do you want to do?"

"I want to go back to school." The words seemed to come out of me without any volition and the clarity of the statement and the conviction of my voice took me by surprise.

"Then register."

Chapter Fifteen

As soon as I went to Pace College in 1970, I became happy again. Naomi was fourteen, Bobby twelve years old now. I started taking psychology classes, because the subject fascinated me.

At that time, many middle-aged women went back to college. Some went for financial reasons. When the man could not support a large family anymore, especially once the children went to college, the wife had to go back to work. Others were divorced and needed to support themselves. And some hadn't finished college, because they got married young and had to raise the children, and wanted to finish it now. No matter why they went back to school, the women were highly motivated and wanted to learn.

I was a dentist who went to college. It was not logical but it made me happy. I studied psychology, philosophy, English, public speaking, arts appreciation. I enjoyed being among young people in academic settings and I had some interesting teachers. My first psychology teacher was Percy Black. He influenced me in choosing psychology as my profession. My other favorite teacher was a nun who was also a psychology professor, Dr. Hart. I also took statistics and experimental psychology in order to get a B.A. in psychology. My life was very, very busy now: I went to college part-time and took two or three courses a semester; I had the children to take care of and was still part of the carpool driving the children to Hebrew School; I stopped volunteering in the hospital but still worked for Hadassah; and I maintained an active social calendar.

Once a friend of ours, a dental surgeon's wife, invited us to the Heart Fund Ball. She worked on the committee. It was an elegant affair, a dinner dance in a country club. Our friend was selling raffle tickets. The grand prize was a trip to Mexico. We bought a few tickets and won the trip. It was such a surprise! I had never won anything before. However, it took many calls to the honorary chairman and to the bank that issued this prize until finally they arranged a trip to Acapulco for us. Away we went.

We stayed for three days in Mexico City. It is a beautiful old city. We went on a nightclub tour. The first stop was a lovely restaurant called "Hacienda Morales." I ordered a steak, which was simple, but it was served with spinach. Within minutes after the waiter cleared our empty plates off the table, I got sick. I didn't know not to eat vegetables in Mexico. One of the men on the tour gave me Pepto-Bismol. I went to the restroom and returned everything I ate. It made me feel better and we continued with the nightclub tour.

I was fascinated. The mariachi music was beautiful and a different kind of music for me. So was the dancing. After some sightseeing, we went to Acapulco. At the hotel, we met some people from Mexico City. They had a car and showed us around the area. The Acapulco Bay is one of the most beautiful sights I ever saw. We met Edith and my brother-in-law there. In the meantime, the people from Mexico City left. Edith and Amos went with us on a boat ride and we saw the divers for the second time. They were a sight to see, jumping into the ocean from a very high cliff! We had a fantastic vacation.

After winning the prize, I was drafted to work for the American Heart Association. Every year we organized a big fundraiser, usually a dinner dance. We made beautiful decorations and sold scores of raffle tickets for good prizes. I worked on this committee as long as it existed in Peekskill. We raised a lot of money.

When I went back to school, the pain over not being able to work in my profession after putting so much time and effort into it eased. I was stimulated and happy. What started as taking some psychology classes without a goal, only for the love of study, turned into pursuing psychology as a career. But I still had to deal with the other source of pain in my life.

A new dentist came to town. Al met Richard and took him under his wing. Al helped him at his office, advised him to marry his girlfriend who still lived in New York City, and he helped Richard to buy a house. Even though they were as different as could be, they became very close.

Richard was an only child who, in my opinion, lived a protected and sheltered life. He was an introvert. Al was an extrovert. Richard wanted his wife to work in the office, but she had worked all her life and would have rather stayed home. Go figure.

We spent a lot of time with Richard and Carol. We went out to dinner together, they came to our house, and we went to theirs. Richard was a good photographer and took many pictures of us. As time went on, it became too much for me. I didn't mind that Al went jogging with Richard and Carol twice a week. He liked to jog and it relaxed him. But I resented that almost every evening, Al spent hours on the telephone with Richard, talking about Richard's office and telling him about his. Al hardly spoke with me and didn't confide anything in me. Out of self-preservation, I became friendly with an Italian couple.

I met them at the Heart Fund ball. Emilia was a poet and Victor was a music teacher and a composer. Emilia was much older than Victor, but he loved her and depended on her. She ran his business and his life. She was a very smart woman in a "womanly" way. Before long, we spent a lot of time together. They became Al's patients and I took piano lessons with Victor.

We went with them to Italy. By now I'd been to Italy several times, but never to Lake Como and never with a native. Emilia was born in a village overlooking the lake. Lake Como is one of the most beautiful places in Europe and visited by many tourists. We had the advantage of getting to know Emilia's family and experience the area from the locals' perspective. It was such a pleasure to visit Emilia's home.

How I wished to see my home again! I remember being in Emilia's house and Emilia telling me what it was like when she was a little girl. I thought, "I will never see my house again," because it was not possible at that t time; the iron curtain was still in full force. I was happy for Emilia, but I felt sad for my own situation. We also spent a week in Abano, a lovely resort, where Al took mud baths for his aching bones while I did much sightseeing.

In 1974, I received my B.A. in psychology with a minor in education from Pace College. But going to graduate school wasn't as straightforward as getting my undergraduate degree.

I'd become aware of a college for foreign students in New York City. The New School for Social Research was organized by refugees from

Germany. They accepted diplomas from Europe and didn't require the GRE test which I already passed. If I had known about this school before, I would not have gone to undergraduate college for four years. This was nagging me. The classes in this school were taught as they were in Europe, in a big auditorium, with hundreds of students listening to the professor. By now, I was used to smaller classes with more interaction between the student and teacher. I could not participate in seminars or discussions in the city, because it was too much commuting. I wasted a year going there before changing to Marist College in Poughkeepsie, which offered a graduate program in psychology. It seemed like an easier commute to drive an hour north instead of taking the train south into the city.

Marist College was a Catholic college, and the chairman of the psychology department was a monk who seemed very approachable and put me at ease. After the second semester, I transferred to another graduate program in psychology in Dobb's Ferry, about forty-five minutes drive from my house. It was run by Mercy College, also a Catholic college, and the chairman of the psychology department was a nun. I liked the classes and most of the teachers. It was a great joy that Dr. Hart, my teacher from Pace College, taught a class there as well.

I got to do a lot of research during those years. One project I carried out together with another woman my age, Marjorie. Her husband worked for IBM and they had five children. She went back to school to help get the children through college. It was difficult for Marjorie to study after being away from college for a long time but, after a while, she did very well. We decided to do a study on how self-actualized women have happier marriages.

We evaluated over fifty women from different walks of life. It was especially interesting to me that some homemakers scored high on the self-actualization scale while some career women did not. My friend, Gloria, a happy housewife, scored high on the self-actualization scale. I took a wide variety of courses and wrote many papers. Naturally, I enjoyed some courses more than others.

In graduate school I met veterans from Vietnam. Our outlook on life was similar. It shows that people who survive terrible things have much in common. One engineer, who worked in Indian Point, became friendly with me. My friend Gloria's husband was his boss. What a small world it is. However, women can be just friends with men, but men cannot be friends with women in this country. In Munich, I had many male friends. We were like family. Most of us lost our family or part of the family. The relations between men and women were different than here.

One day in the winter, when I did research for a term paper, I took it to the Yorktown campus for Marjorie. As I walked back to the car I slipped on ice and hurt my ankle. Luckily, it was the left leg. So I drove myself to the hospital in Peekskill. While I was in the waiting room, a doctor we were friendly with saw me, took a peek at my ankle and said, "It looks broken." Meanwhile, the x-ray showed nothing and I was dismissed. At home I was in terrible pain. My leg was swollen and I could not step on it. We were having a snowstorm at the time. Everything was closed and we were snowed in. The next day I made an appointment with the orthopedic doctor in Al's medical building. This time the x-ray showed a hairline fracture. The doctor put a plaster shoe on to immobilize the foot, and it stopped hurting. My agony was over. My years in graduate school at Mercy College were good in spite of a broken ankle. Our thesis on the correlation between self-actualization and marriage was a splendid success.

I received my Master's degree in psychology in 1978. It was a beautiful summer day. Al and the children and Mother came to the graduation. Naomi graduated from Ithaca College that summer – Magna cum Laude – and Bob was studying at SUNY College at Oneonta then. So my daughter and I graduated at the same time. Mother was very proud of me. Both she and Father were always supportive and encouraged me to study.

Cousin Mira had just lost her husband, Dr. Simon Gitelson, in Israel, and came to be with Mother and us. We all went together to Naomi's graduation. We were very proud of her. Another chapter of my life had finished and a new one begun.

Chapter Sixteen

AL CONTINUED TO BE A very busy man. He was an excellent dentist, a good administrator, and still the president of the medical building. It took much of his time and effort. Things like plumbing, air conditioning, landscaping, and other issues had to be taken care of. Dr. David Lack, the treasurer, was a big help. Al had an outstanding relationship with his patients and his staff. His patients always came first and he would do anything for them. He treated the dentists and hygienists as well as the assistants and office staff as friends, not as employees. Many young dentists who worked for him later opened their own offices and did very well. Having worked for Dr. Genis was an excellent reference.

Al loved Peekskill. He went hiking with three male friends, jogging with Richard and Carol, ice skating to Bear Mountain, which was close to us, and he'd joined a skating club on Sundays. He was a good skater and taught the children and later the grandchildren to ice skate. Al was also an officer at the Jewish Center and was involved in different community projects. He was also president of the local Dental Society for two years. He had such a wonderful way with people and could get along with anyone. There was nobody who didn't like Al Genis. So Al, the partisan, was a hero in peace time also.

Fortunately I was busy, too. Throughout school I had kept up my involvement with Hadassah and some other community projects, as well as our lively social calendar and my gardening. As soon as I received my Master's Degree, I began looking for a job. But nothing was available in my area. So I went to the Mental Health Clinic on Washington Street in Peekskill and offered to work as a volunteer. The clinic consisted of four social workers, one psychiatrist, and one psychologist who was leading groups. The person in charge, a Puerto Rican woman named Margarita, was a social worker. She accepted me to work in the clinic as a volunteer. I got to do therapy just like the psychiatric social workers. Once a week, we discussed the cases. The whole staff, including the psychiatrist, Dr. Murphy, was present. I was not paid, but was learning a lot and enjoying it.

In the beginning, Dr. Murphy was skeptical of me and seemed to think I was a dentist, not a psychologist. But over time he came to value me and expressed much respect for my approach to the patients. One of the social workers, a Jewish woman from Vienna, was especially critical.

For example, I worked with a divorced woman who was raising a son by herself and experienced a great many difficulties. The boy was extremely disruptive and manipulative and his mother was unable to handle him. I was supposed to teach her how to discipline him, but she didn't catch on. My critical colleague couldn't understand why we didn't make more progress and was very verbal about this.

"The boy is all she has," I explained. "That's why he's able to take advantage of her."

Another case of mine was a woman who kept fantasizing about running away. I tried to explain her predicament, but my Viennese critic couldn't understand it and spoke to me as if I encouraged my patient to run away. Fortunately, Margarita, Dr. Murphy, and my other colleagues valued my work, and no matter what, I always remained on the side of the patient.

Naomi, who had graduated from college that year, was accepted to many universities and picked UCLA for her graduate studies. Since she went into public health, she decided to take an internship in Phelps Hospital in Tarrytown, close to Peekskill, and to stay with us. It was her last summer at home. Harold, a friend of hers from high school though a few years older than Naomi, spent the summer in Long Island with his mother and stepfather. Harold's aunt lived next door to us and when he found out that Naomi was home, he called her. They started spending much time together and they fell in love. We were not aware of their feelings for each other, but I liked Harold right from the beginning.

One evening, not long after Naomi had moved to Los Angeles, the phone rang when we were in bed already. It was Naomi. There is a difference in time of three hours between LA and New York.

"Mommy, I'm engaged," she said.

"To whom?" I replied.

"To Harold."

"Oh, that's wonderful! Congratulations!"

We were surprised but very happy that our Naomi was getting engaged to a nice boy. The wedding was the next September on Labor Day weekend. I made all the wedding arrangements and it was an extraordinary pleasure for me. I did not have a pretty wedding, but my daughter had a beautiful wedding. After their honeymoon in Jamaica, Naomi went back to UCLA to finish her studies while Harold got a job in Los Angeles. A year, later Naomi graduated and received her Master's degree. Then Harold decided to become a chiropractor and went to Chiropractic College while Naomi worked. They moved to Santa Monica.

Before Christmas of 1979, Margarita called me to her office and asked me to be the chairman of the "Presents for Patients" drive. They did it every year and this year I was made responsible. The clinic was run by the State and most patients were poor and needed all the support they could get. I threw myself into this project full force and it was an immense success. Many organizations donated for the patients. At the same time, Al and I were nominated by the Jewish Center to receive an award for the State of Israel Bonds. The plaque for Albert and Alice Genis, dated December 1979, hangs proudly in my living room. Both events were announced in the local newspaper at the same time. Both events took much work and preparation.

Even though I loved my work in the clinic, I kept looking for a paid job. It wasn't as much about the money as it was about wanting the recognition of being a professional after all the hard work I had put into my studies. So when I read in the newspaper about on opening for an assistant psychologist in Pines Bridge School in Yorktown, which was part of an organization named BOCES, I applied. I got called to an interview and was accepted.

Pines Bridge School was a school for mentally handicapped children. My job was to evaluate these children, which included taking their IQ, as well as supporting the teachers and the parents. It was not easy to work in these surroundings, but I loved the children. Most of them had Down Syndrome. The brighter ones had an IQ of fifty, others lower than that. My boss was not around much. He went to a lot of meetings and I was left there to do the work, but I didn't mind. I liked my job.

In the spring of 1980 Bobby graduated from college. Mother, Naomi, Al, and I went to the graduation. It was such a happy occasion.

However, once again, things didn't go smoothly for me. In the summer of 1980, the administration at BOCES made some big changes. They combined the social work department with the psychology department and my position was cut. So I lost my job.

Fortunately, we had plans to travel to Europe. Our tour was a week in France and a week in Switzerland. I'd been in Switzerland before with Al and the Dental Society from New York. At that time we visited Zurich, Geneva, and other beautiful places in Switzerland. This time we stayed in the mountains in a village called Farchant, one hour from St. Moritz. It was a fabulous week. We went for long walks into the mountains and we went to a polka party where we danced all night. It took only one hour to go to St Moritz by bus and the buses ran every hour. They were so punctual that one could set one's watch accordingly. So we went to St Moritz a few times. It is a lovely resort town. The week in France was different, but just as delightful. We were lucky to have the opportunity to upgrade our hotel for $100 and got to stay close to the Eiffel Tower, not in the outskirts like the other participants of the tour. We very much enjoyed a boat ride on the River Seine and a bus tour to the Cathedral of Chartre and to chalet country. So life had some good and some bad in store once more. To lose my first paid job as a psychologist was hard on me, but I took great pleasure in our travels and began thinking about what to do next.

Because I'd loved school since I was a young girl and loved working with children, and because I could build on my Master's in psychology, I decided to continue with school psychology. Because of my poor health, I had to look for a college close to home, and I found the College of New Rochelle. They had a sixty credits school psychology program and certification, which meant it was difficult to get into this college. I gathered my degrees and referrals from previous teachers along with my resume and was very excited when I was invited to an interview with the chairman of the department and a teacher. I was accepted!

In addition to the courses, I had to do internships in schools. I worked in the elementary school at Lake Mohegan and another semester in a middle school. It took two intense years of study to get the certification as a school psychologist.

One day, in 1981, I received a distressing phone call from Edith.

"Mira is dead," Edith said, her voice choked. "I read about her in the Jerusalem Post. She was murdered."

"Are you sure? What happened?" I answered, stunned.

Edith read me the entire article. To this day it upsets me to think about how hard Cousin Mira's life was: How she suffered in several concentration camps; how she lived her life childless with a brilliant but difficult husband who refused to adopt when they couldn't have children; how she mourned him deeply when he died and lived with Mother for a while in New York, unable to work in her profession as a nurse for quite some time – only to be killed by her plumber in her own home in Jerusalem.

"How are we going to tell Mother?" I asked, after composing myself. Mira had been like a third daughter to our mother.

"I don't know," Edith replied.

We didn't have to figure it out. Mother also subscribed to the Jerusalem Post and called us soon after. The news hit her hard as well.

Yet life has a way of its own, and in February of 1983, one of Al's and my greatest joys happened: Naomi gave birth to a beautiful baby boy, our first grandchild. We almost missed Ryan's Bris because of a snowstorm. For two long nights we slept at the airport before finally being on our way. A friend of Naomi's picked us up from the airport in Los Angeles, and they actually had to make the Moel wait.

From then on, I went to visit Naomi and her family twice a year, sometimes with, sometimes without Al. I loved traveling over there; six hours on a plane while I ate a meal and watched a movie, and there I was. It was a vacation to me, especially in the winter when I left the harsh Northeastern cold behind and enjoyed the mild climate of Southern California. I fondly remember taking Ryan for a stroll in his baby carriage on Ocean Avenue, and stopping for a croissant and coffee. One year, while I visited Mother in Florida, Al went to California by himself to spend time with Naomi. The two of them were always very close.

When I received the school psychologist's certification in 1983, I looked for work in the schools, but there were no openings whatsoever in the greater Peekskill region. So I went back to BOCES and worked in the guidance department. The majority of the job consisted of testing and evaluating the IQ of students and writing reports to the schools. Even though every school employed a school psychologist, in special cases the psychologist from the guidance center had to come in and do the testing. The other part of my job was to replace school psychologists who were out on maternity or sick leave. I helped out in an elementary school and in the middle school in Putnam Valley, which were middle class suburban schools. What sticks in my memory most is working in Peekskill Elementary School. This was an inner city school where the children were disruptive. I worked with a good teacher who had a very difficult class. My job was to help her manage the class. Most children came from homes without fathers. It was a completely different world from what I knew. I felt sorry for the teacher and the children who did not have normal childhoods and took it out on others. I could relate to them, because even though I had loving parents, I also didn't have a normal childhood. I think the main reason I was drawn to working with children was my lost youth. My hope and faith helped me before and now made me go on and on. I was trying to make something out of myself, to accomplish something, and to lead a full and meaningful life. I did the best I could to inspire these children. However, it was draining, and when there was an opening in a school outside of the inner city environment, I grabbed it.

Around this time, I also became president of Hadassah. I had been involved in Hadassah for years, but had not taken the presidency before because I was too busy with school. Now I had no excuse to refuse anymore. I enjoyed it tremendously. We were a good team and I developed many friendships while supporting the Hadassah Hospital in Jerusalem, which helps all people alike, Jews and Arabs and everybody who needs medical treatment.

It was rewarding and enjoyable, a welcome change from study for many years. I didn't know I had the talent to do this kind of work, to conduct meetings and to supervise fundraising. Thankfully, I had much help and support from the officers and the membership. Once a month I wrote a message for the bulletin. I liked to do it and the girls liked to read it. When I first came to America, I was shy about speaking English to anyone, and for a long time I was still shy about speaking in public but, thanks to my practice speaking in college and graduate school, I now enjoyed speaking to an audience. Of course, I prepared my speeches in advance. This is a very useful and important part of American education, to be able to write well and to speak well. I received several awards from our chapter and from the Westchester region.

Once again, I was extremely busy. I remember trying to write my reports for BOCES and the phone wouldn't stop ringing with people from Hadassah. After every interruption, it would take me a while to find my focus again. So someone suggested I should get an answering machine. What a superb idea that was!

While I was president of Hadassah the first time, two very happy events took place: In May of 1983, Bobby graduated from the Syracuse University College of Law and was hired right out of school into a prestigious law firm in New York City. A neighbor of ours had relatives who owned an apartment building in Brooklyn Heights, so that's where Bobby moved. It was a charming section of Brooklyn, mostly young people – so-called Yuppies – lived there and we very much enjoyed visiting our son in the city.

In December of 1984, Naomi gave birth to our second grandchild. Al and I traveled to California to help out. Harold took Naomi to the hospital Christmas night and we stayed home with Ryan, who was only two years old. Our happiness was indescribable when the phone rang just after midnight and Harold told us that a little girl named Brittany had arrived and both mother and child were healthy. Al and I stayed a couple of weeks and it was an incredible pleasure for me to be able to be there for Naomi like Mother had been for me when Naomi was born.

When Al and I returned to Peekskill, we resumed our busy lives. Al began thinking of slowing down and contemplated selling the office to some of the younger dentists and work as an employee. Meanwhile, I worked countless hours for Hadassah, and my job at BOCES was demanding and tiresome. I had to move from one school to the other and never had my own office. I remember having to take my lunch break in the school cafeteria, surrounded by rambunctious and noisy children.

It may have been lunch, but it certainly wasn't much of a break. Even though I never got paid for my volunteer work at the Mental Health Clinic, working there had felt more like a real job than this did. Then something happened that once again changed the direction of my career path.

Al treated many patients who suffered from temporomandibular joint dysfunction – TMJ – an involuntary and automatic process. Aside from troubles with their teeth, these patients were afflicted with painful spasms, bad headaches, and even earaches. Al fitted them with an appliance to wear while sleeping to prevent teeth grinding. He became very interested in TMJ, took courses, and discovered biofeedback therapy as a possible treatment modality. It is a clinical procedure whereby patients are taught to monitor certain physiological responses and then, through training, develop the skill to exercise voluntary control of these processes. This is done by using sensitive electronic instrumentation. Among the professionals who took these workshops and became biofeedback therapists were doctors, nurses, and psychologists. So for me it was a natural fit and I took to it like a fish to water. Through the Biofeedback Association, I met a man who sold the instruments required for biofeedback and ran classes in his house, which was in Ossining, not far from Peekskill. I took whatever workshops he offered as well as several courses through other organizations and various colleges, including an advanced training program in clinical biofeedback from the Institute for Psychosomatic Research.

And then in 1985, after all those years of Al keeping me away from his dental practice, he converted a small room there into an office for me and I started working with some of his patients, using biofeedback techniques to assist in the treatment of their TMJ. I'd completed my first time as president of Hadassah after two years. Of course, I remained involved as a volunteer, but my load lightened considerably and I was able to put much energy into my new career. My success was instant and I adored my little office, and I loved working one-on-one with my patients. With my first paycheck, I bought myself a new piano! Soon I not only treated men and women with TMJ dysfunction, but people with migraines and tension headaches, irritable bowel syndrome, ulcers, anxieties, phobias, and a variety of stress-related disorders. As per some requirements, I needed to either have a PhD or have a PhD psychologist supervise me. So I found a man who qualified in White Plains and, once a month or so, I went to his house and presented my cases to him. He marveled at my success rate which was quite a bit higher than his. What made my approach so successful, I believe, was the combination of biofeedback methods and psychology. As before, I treated every patient like a person, and I still feel the most important aspect of the treatment is the relationship of the therapist with the patient. Many of my patients were middle-aged women whose situation I could relate to very well.

But before long, Al sold the business to a husband-and-wife-dentist team and began working for them as an employee. I started paying rent to the new owners, and then they needed my room and moved me downstairs. I still very much enjoyed the work, but it wasn't as pleasant anymore as when I felt like part of the professional team in the office. Not much time passed until they said they needed the downstairs office as well and asked me to vacate it. Al was very helpful and immediately offered to transform his study in our home into an office where I could see patients.

Today the treatment of TMJ dysfunction has become commonplace and many dentists specialize in it exclusively, but Al was a pioneer in this field. I continued taking classes and later completed a difficult exam and became a board-certified biofeedback therapist. In 1987, we bought a condominium in South Florida and, in 1988, we began spending some time there in the winters. My friends from Hadassah approached me and, to make a long story short, I became president again from 1988 to 1991.

The lives of our children continued to change as well. To our great joy, Naomi, Harold, and their children moved back east, closer to the family. Harold got a job as a chiropractor in Rockland County. Initially, Naomi didn't work – she had her hands full with the two children anyway – but soon she found part-time employment as a teacher in a Jewish center. Before long, Harold started his own practice in Brewster. Al helped them find the office, and Naomi became Harold's receptionist and office manager.

Bobby had joined another law firm where he had met his future wife, Sherri. She was not only helpful to him in the new firm, she was also instrumental in finding him an apartment in Manhattan. One day Bobby visited us and discussed the possibility of starting his own law firm. Al was all for it and told Bobby to go ahead, not to be afraid, and to do it as soon as possible, while he was still young and enthusiastic. It gave Al and me enormous pleasure to see how much Bobby loved his profession. He took his father's advice and didn't wait long, and he asked Sherri to join him as a partner. Soon Sonin & Genis was founded; Bobby, ever the gentleman, explained, "Ladies first." They started out modestly in the Bronx, where they rented a room in another lawyer's office.

A short time later, in 1989, they got married. Sherri's mother arranged the wedding. It took place in Long Island and was very, very luxurious. We held the Aufruf in Peekskill and hosted a lovely party at the Colonial Terrace where many of our family events had taken place, including Bobby's Bar Mitzvah, Naomi's wedding, and a surprise party I had organized for Al's sixtieth birthday.

Even though Mother was aging and had been for a while, everybody who knew her said what a lady she was. She was still beautiful and carried herself very gracefully at Bobby's wedding, was sharp, sophisticated, and most of all still as kind as ever. She had moved to a senior citizen development close to Edith in Chicago in 1983. Initially this was very painful for me, but over time I came to understand and accept her decision.

First of all Mother never liked Peekskill. And who could blame her – neither did I! Edith, however, loved where she lived, in Highland Park, a suburb of Chicago, and so did Mother. Secondly, Al and I took advantage of every opportunity we got to travel, so Mother was concerned that she would be alone in Peekskill more than if she lived near Edith. And last but not least, it was only natural that Edith and Mother were somewhat closer than I was with Mother. I got married and left home early, while Edith lived with Mother much longer, and then they went to America together before Al and I did. But no matter how much I came to terms with Mother's decision to move away, I always missed Mother very much and continued talking with her almost every morning. Fortunately she came to visit us often. Her grandchildren adored her as did everybody who knew her.

Mother's health had always been fragile, like mine, and by now she had diabetes, a serious heart condition, and her kidneys were failing and she was on dialysis, which in those days was not as common as it is today. The doctor suggested for her to be put into a nursing home.

I Won't Die Hungry

Edith wouldn't hear of it. We knew how much Mother loved her little apartment. So Edith put an ad for a nursing assistant in the Polish paper. Edith received over a hundred responses, and Mother took an immediate liking to a lovely woman named Wanda. The only problem was that Wanda didn't drive. But Edith made it work and drove Mother to dialysis herself.

And then in the winter of 1991, I received a call that Mother was feeling worse and had been hospitalized with pneumonia. I got on a plane as soon as I could. Edith had come down with pneumonia as well, so I slept at Cousin Elliot's house, Aunt Hanna and Uncle Moshe's son. Mother was weak when I got there, but before long she seemed to improve. So I went back to Peekskill, where my patients and other obligations were waiting for me.

I'll never forget the morning after my return to Peekskill. Before leaving the house, I called the hospital. Instead of Mother, Edith answered the phone.

"Mother is dead," she sobbed.

How can I describe the pain I felt, we all felt? Everybody loved our mother, especially her grandchildren. Naomi had always referred to her grandma as her favorite person and I often suspected that Naomi loved my mother more than she loved me.

Many people came to the funeral in Chicago, family and friends from far and near, including some of our friends from Vilno and from Munich who live in Chicago now. Edith had ordered a beautiful, red coffin, and Mother looked very pretty in it, all made-up, like they do it here in America. She still looked like a lady. Several people spoke about her, including me, and many wonderful things were said. Among them were how she took care of her second husband for years until his death in 1974 when she wasn't even well herself, and how they'd called her "Schwester Miriam" in Föhrenwald where she had delivered over five-hundred babies. What was repeated over and over again was how she always helped everyone she possibly could.

She had wanted to be buried in Chicago. Edith's husband's family had a plot there, and Mother felt this way there would always be someone to take care of the grave. Her second husband was buried in New York in a cemetery that was hard to get to and, of course, Father was buried back in Munich. It still hurts to think of my grandparents and Uncle

Mula who were killed in the Gleboki Ghetto and never got a funeral. Yet at least we know where they died; even worse off are people like Uncle Lipa's family who were simply gone without a trace. I marvel sometimes when I see at the Peekskill cemetery how many whole families are buried in the same graveyard.

But even Mother's burial wasn't without complications. The ground was frozen under a thick layer of snow, and there was a strike, so they couldn't put her into the earth until several weeks after the official funeral.

I remember how heartbroken I was for a long time. For months, every morning I realized anew that I couldn't call her anymore, and profound sadness overcame me. For a while, I felt angry at Edith because she had taken Mother away for all those years, but in time I let go of those feelings and soon Edith and I grew close and became friends. I suppose there must have always been some rivalry between us, and now it had become unnecessary to compete with each other. To this day Edith and I speak on the phone almost every day, and we both will treasure the memory of our beloved parents for as long as we live.

Al and I at brunch while visiting Naomi and Harold in Santa Monica, California (Early 1980's)

Al and I on a Mediterranean Cruise.
(1992)

Chapter Seventeen

IN THE LATE FALL OF 1992, Al and I went on a marvelous Mediterranean cruise. We had gone on a cruise in Scandinavia before where we joined a club that made cruises relatively inexpensive.

After flying to Nice and staying there overnight, a bus took us to Monaco, where Grace Kelly and Prince Rainier had lived. It was a very enjoyable trip through enchanting scenery and we stopped at a perfume factory. A seductive scent hung in the air, and the bottles lined up on the shelves looked like oversized diamonds filled with promising potions. Nobody left without a fancy bag containing at least one fragrance in their hands.

Then we spent a night in glamorous Monaco. They didn't allow people in casual attire into the casinos, especially women in casual slacks. It had to be dress pants or dresses. So many of us, including Al and I, didn't get in. That didn't bother us. We enjoyed ourselves going for a walk in the elegant city instead and ate in an excellent restaurant.

The next day we boarded the ship. Our first stop was in Italy, in Laverne, a port city not far from Florence. Since Al and I had been to Florence before, we joined the alternate tour to Tuscany. I loved the picturesque landscape and I remember how it rained lightly when we saw the leaning tower of Pisa. Coming from America, I expected the tower to be tall and was surprised by how small it was.

The next place we got off the ship was Naples. Together with another couple, we rented a taxi. I had never imagined that Naples was such a pretty city. It reminded me of Haifa. From Naples, the ship took us to Greece. Even though it was the beginning of November already, the climate had been pleasant everywhere. However, a strong wind blew during the one-day trip from Italy to Greece on the Adriatic Sea and made it quite a shaky journey. I got seasick for the first time in my life and had to lie down.

We stopped in Turkey and saw Ephesus, an ancient city that disappeared like Pompeii. Only the ruins remained, but we could see what a beautiful city it had been. It was very impressive.

Once we got to Greece, it was warm and felt like summer. They stored little boats on the ship and had us climb in and then slowly lowered us down to the ocean's surface. Being in these tiny boats on the vast, sparkling blue sea was a most exquisite experience and, thankfully, I didn't get seasick anymore. We visited several islands that way, including Santorini, Mykonos, and Rhodes. I remember Santorini best. Its little town was high up on a mountain top and we had to ride on donkeys to get up there. The view was spectacular.

We stayed three days in Athens which was marvelous, too. Not as big as Rome, but also filled with interesting museums and beautiful ancient architecture. In one of the museums, together with another couple, we hired a private guide. He gave us an excellent lecture in English on the history of Greek art, which I enjoyed very much. One night we visited a nightclub, where we met some people from South Africa. They were white and called themselves Afrikaners. Al and I found their accents quite peculiar. On our last day, we went to the Byzantium museum, which was also extremely fascinating.

Then we flew to Israel from an airport that was very different from any other airport I had ever been to. People flew from here to Egypt, Israel, and other middle-Eastern countries. It was crazy, crowded, and noisy, and quite the experience. The flight from Athens to Tel Aviv took only one hour and we spent nine days in Israel. We had such a lovely time, visiting family and friends. One of the memories that stands out from that trip was the get-together with an old friend of Al's from his small hometown, Plissa. This man had been a partisan also. Actually, he was the fellow I mentioned who wouldn't shoot the German spy because she was unarmed. He had remained in Russia and married a woman from Minsk and they'd come to Israel with five sons.

Not long after our return from Europe, the year 1992 ended with an extraordinary joy. We were in Florida, at a New Year's party at our friend Slava's house, the woman who had survived being buried alive in a pit as

I Won't Die Hungry

a young girl. We mingled in her back yard, and I loved being outside at this time of the year. I remember how balmy the air was when someone handed me the phone. It was Bobby. His first child, Isaiah, our third grandchild, had been born.

About a year later, when we returned from spending some time in Florida again, Al wasn't feeling well. He said it was just a cold and went back to work right away. But I saw he was ill. Finally, he went to his internist, one of the partners in the medical building. Al was told that there was nothing wrong with him, that he was working too hard and just needed a vacation. He did work a lot, but as soon as he came home, he'd lie down immediately. In the morning his temperature was normal, whereas every evening he had a low grade fever, and he continued to cough very badly. The coughing was what worried me the most. Finally, a few weeks later, the doctor sent Al to the hospital for x-rays. Evidently, the x-ray didn't show anything, but they followed up with an MRI and found cancer in the kidney.

When Al told me he had cancer, I started yelling and screaming. I felt like my world was falling apart.

"You should have gone to the doctor sooner," I screamed. "You shouldn't have waited that long."

As soon as I recovered from the shock, I started to make telephone calls. We knew an oncologist who had been a patient of Al's since he was a little boy. He knew an excellent surgeon at Sloan Kettering Cancer Center, and I immediately made an appointment. But Al wanted to be treated by the chairman, so after a few more phone calls, we got an appointment with the chairman and his team. They were worried about the lungs, so they did more tests and found that the cancer had already spread to the lungs.

Two doctors operated on Al at the same time. The chairman took out Al's kidney tumor and a young woman worked on his lungs. She'd come to see him before the surgery and, for some reason, as soon as I saw her I had a bad feeling about the whole thing.

The operation took six hours which felt like an eternity to me. Naomi and Bobby stayed with me in the waiting room hour after hour after hour. By the time the surgeon called us in, I was convinced he was going to tell us Al was dead. The fear I was experiencing was as bad as any fear I can remember. What a relief it was when the surgeon reported that both the kidney tumor and the lung tumor had been removed successfully. However, he said that the lung surgeon wasn't sure if some cancer cells survived in the remaining tissues.

Al surprised doctors, friends, and family alike in how quickly he recovered. We took him home just before the 4th of July. It was such a wonderful holiday for us! Edith came to visit and, together with the children, we celebrated the occasion joyously on our patio. Having Al with us again, we experienced everything with renewed appreciation: the warmth of the sun on our skin; the gentle wind whispering in the tree branches above us; the magnificent colors of peonies and the lush green of the grass; the smell from the barbecue and the taste of the plentiful food on our plates; and, at the end of the day, the fireworks sparkling in the velvety sky. We felt a great sense of hope that all would be fine.

During the next three months, Al continued to recover remarkably well. He went for walks in the neighborhood. In those days everybody still knew everybody. Nobody looking at Al could believe that he had just lived through a six-hour surgery. Before long, we began babysitting for the children again. Somehow they often seemed to need us at the same time. I remember one weekend, when Naomi and Harold were out of town, Bobby and Sherri got installed as officers of the Jewish Lawyers Guild, at the Jewish Museum and needed us to take care of their baby for a few hours. We ended up hiring a babysitter for Ryan and Brittany, and Al drove us back and forth between the two residences so we could take care of Isaiah. Soon afterwards we celebrated Bobby's 35th birthday in a restaurant in Manhattan. We felt very optimistic.

But then, when he went for a follow-up scan, the test showed cancer cells in the lungs. Immediately, we called Sloan Kettering. They confirmed the findings from our hospital in Peekskill. The prognosis was poor. The surgeon suggested an experimental test group that was run at Sloan Kettering for men age sixty to seventy.

Initially, Al did well with the experimental drug. Every evening I gave him an injection of the chemo. But after a few weeks the treatment took its toll and he grew weaker and weaker. His oncologist said it was okay for us to spend the winter in Florida and recommended an oncologist there. For a short time Al improved again, then he stayed the same for a while, and finally he regressed. We returned to Peekskill in the spring. Soon it was summer and a very hard summer it was for us. Several times

Al had to be hospitalized at Sloan Kettering, which is located in New York City. The city seemed especially hot and humid that year. I stayed with Al at the hospital during the day and with Bobby and Sherri at night. Sherri had just given birth to Mariah, our fourth grandchild. Naomi and Harold, too, were extremely supportive and, when they couldn't, Al's friends and colleagues drove us to the city. It was during that time that I stopped seeing patients for good.

One evening, I went home to Peekskill to relax for a day. When I stepped out onto our patio after yet another scorching and noisy day in the city, I suddenly noticed how wonderful and peaceful the country was. The trees towered above me and I savored their sheltering shade. I took a breath of the fresh air and realized how lucky I was to live here. It was the first time that I fully appreciated my home. Before I had always thought how unhappy I was there.

As I walked back into the house, I remembered all the good times we had had here. It was hard to believe that Al was deathly ill now. I thought about Bomka, the boy I had fallen in love with when I was a teenager, before the horrors of the war started, the boy who was liked by all, and who became a famous partisan – who then became Al, the athletic, positive, and outgoing man, again liked by all. It seemed whatever he touched was successful. So that's what I focused on when I crawled into bed by myself that night. With all the strength I could muster up I maintained hope that he would survive. Despite our difficulties at times, I simply could not imagine life without him.

One day in the early fall when Al was back at home, impulsively and without thinking, I said, "I always wanted to go back to Vilno to see my house, and you didn't want to. Now I will never see the house again."

"Go now with your sister," Al answered.

I told him I didn't want to leave him alone at this time, but he insisted.

"I want you to go," he said until I called Edith.

She agreed immediately and suggested we also visit Budapest and Prague. So I called our travel agent in New York, an Israeli and distant cousin of Al's who had organized several trips for us before. In record time everything fell into place and Edith and I were on our way to see the house I had said goodbye to when I was thirteen years old.

Chapter Eighteen

OUR FIRST STOP WAS IN Budapest, a picturesque city divided in two by the Danube. Even though we got to see the Dohany Street Synagogue only from the outside – as it was under construction – it was very memorable. As far as I know, even at the time of this writing, it is still the second largest synagogue in the world. Both Edith and I were delighted to have the opportunity to go to the opera while in Budapest. It was a Hungarian folk opera whose title escapes me, but it was very pretty.

From there we traveled to Prague which is filled with much Jewish history. We visited the old synagogue and the new synagogue and walked a lot. I liked that city; it reminded me of Munich after the war, and even of Vilno a little bit. What stays in my mind more than anything is the so-called Children's Museum. People from all over the world come to see it. It houses a collection of drawings by the Jewish children from Theresienstadt[8] and to this day I can see some of the pictures in my mind's eye.

From Prague we went to Warsaw. Here we visited the historic ghetto, where a few young people dared to rise up against the German army on April 19, 1943. These few brave souls fought the strongest army in Europe. They knew they didn't have a chance, but they decided to die with honor, not to go like sheep to the slaughter. It seemed to Edith and me as if we saw the blood in the streets. We figured out that we were in the Pushcha during that time, after escaping from Gleboki Ghetto,

---

8 A concentration camp, also known as Terezin, located in what is now the Czech Republic

before settling in Golducha. Al had been fighting with the partisans for over a year already.

On May 16, 1943, Mordechai Anielewicz, the leader of the uprising, committed suicide together with his wife, Mira, and a group of comrades in the headquarter's bunker. Officially the uprising was over; however, fighting continued until June, 1943 and some people survived in the sewer system until 1944.

A year after the Warsaw Ghetto Uprising, the historic Polish Uprising took place. The Russians were on the outskirts of Warsaw already, but didn't get involved in the fighting and, ultimately, let the Germans destroy the city of Warsaw. But in 1994, when we were there, it was completely rebuilt. Where the ghetto used to be were apartment buildings now. Only in a small designated area, we saw two monuments. One represented men, women, and children fighting, the other one was for Mordechai Anielewicz.

The Warsaw Ghetto Uprising is considered one of the most important events in Jewish history. To many Jews, myself included, the uprising symbolizes a turning point from passivity to fighting back. It was the beginning of a new nation.

Finally, we flew to Vilno which is called Vilnius now. A tourist guide and a driver met us at the airport to take us to our hotel. The guide spoke English and pointed out the main streets. They had different names now, but I remembered each and every one of them; it all came back. I could feel my heartbeat in my chest as we drove through the whole city, and it started beating faster and faster when we approached the Green Bridge, close to where we used to live. Every morning on my way to school, I crossed that bridge! The guide told us that the original bridge had been destroyed by bombs and had been rebuilt during the communist regime. He pointed to a monument of a soldier and a worker and a farmer. Right then he could have showed me a statue by Michelangelo and it wouldn't have interested me. I knew that as soon as we crossed the bridge, I would be able to see our house. Edith and I craned our necks and squeezed each other's hands, and suddenly, there it was. There, on a little hill, stood our house, just as beautiful as I remembered it. What a sight this was! But before we knew it, the driver turned left and our house disappeared behind us again. The guide explained that we needed to check in at the hotel first.

I Won't Die Hungry

The twenty-some floor building was relatively new and had been built by the Soviets. It was called Hotel Lietuva. Our steps echoed through an extremely large and totally empty lobby. The guide registered us and we were escorted to our room. A woman who'd been introduced to us as the maid displayed a bossy demeanor and told us to call her if we needed anything. The room was cold and we couldn't get the heating to work, so we let her know about it. She made one call, again sounding very authoritative and, immediately, we were moved to another room. Later, we found out that the maids at this hotel had previously worked for the KGB.

The next morning, we began three days of intense sightseeing with our tour guide. We covered much of the city by foot. Edith was glad that she had listened to me and taken a warm coat. Initially, she'd only packed a fall jacket. She didn't remember that October over there is much cooler than in New York or Chicago. People were wearing long coats, hats, scarves, and gloves, and looked decent overall. I was very comfortable in my woolen beret and my raincoat whose thick and fluffy lining kept me warm.

The tour guide soon realized that this was "our" city; after all, we were born here. What was new to us were the street names, which were Lithuanian now and had been Polish when we lived here. This was interesting to him, since he remembered the Russian street names which came into effect after the war and had only been changed to Lithuanian since Lithuania had gained independence.

It was strange to walk down the main street which used to be so lively, lined with cafes and theaters. Many an evening our parents took us here for a stroll. The only worthwhile attraction now was a big grocery store. It had a self-serve cafeteria and in the evening, Edith and I returned here for dinner. We were curious about what people ate nowadays, and I remember enjoying a generous portion of smoked fish. For some reason, people sold grapes on the street and tiny bananas, which must have been imported. We took some back with us to the hotel room.

More than anything, of course, we wanted to go into our house. When Helene, Edith's daughter, had traveled here, Vilno still belonged to the Soviet Union and the Singer House was used by the party. No one was allowed in at that time.

It felt like a dream when we finally walked up the beautiful staircase into my grandfather's apartment. The staircase with its rounded walls and wide steps made of white marble had not changed at all. I'd been so impatient to get here, but now I slowed right down to savor every step. Edith's eyes were huge, and both of us spoke in a hushed voice as if mindful of a majestic presence.

Even though, intellectually, I thought I was prepared for anything, I gasped when we entered our grandfather's apartment. I suppose because the staircase looked and felt exactly as I remembered it, my grandfather's apartment being an office came as a shock to me. All of the old furniture was gone. Like soldiers frozen in time, rows of stark desks filled the place and filing cabinets lined the walls. But when I looked up, I recognized the beautifully ornate ceiling, and Edith pointed to the parquet floors which had also remained the same. Ever so slowly we made our way into what used to be the salon and lingered at the tower which was still like before. We walked over to Aunt Celia's room which had a small balcony overlooking the garden. Despite its now dreary appearance, my mind's eye could see blooming acacias and lilac bushes and almost smell their lovely fragrance.

From there we went to Aunt Frieda and Uncle Lipa's apartment downstairs, which was laid out exactly like my grandfather's apartment. A charming restaurant was there now, with small tables and chairs. Proud and excited the guide informed us about the widespread development of private enterprise, now that the new regime allowed private business. After we sat down and ordered coffee, his voice faded into background noise for me. I was transported into another time.

It is 1941. Vilno is under German occupation. This beautiful house catches their eye and they establish their headquarters here. They draft a young German language teacher and get him to work as an interpreter. This was the young man from whom I took English lessons in Munich after the war. I remember eating up his words when he told me about working in the Singer House.

In 1944 the Soviets take over Vilno. They too fancy this marvelous building and make it theirs immediately. Nobody but party officials and office workers are allowed inside these walls for decades. And now, fifty years later, the Lithuanians are in control and are changing the function of this building once again.

As I sat in Uncle Lipa's apartment, sipping hot coffee, I felt that this beautiful house had essentially remained the same. Like a grand dame, it withstood everything and continued to stand tall and proud with old charm and elegance.

The memory of Uncle Lipa and his family came back in a very different way the next day. Our guide took us to Ponary, the infamous place of mass murder where 100,000 human beings had been killed, of them 70,000 Jews, among them Uncle Lipa's family and so many others of our family, friends, and neighbors. I thought of Cousin Gita, who'd been four months younger than I. She was an only child and very neat. Among other toys, she had the most beautiful little tea set I'd ever seen. We had many tea parties in her room. Most people who lived in our house found their end here, and if we hadn't left that fateful night, we would have, too.

Ponary was one of the eeriest sights I've ever set my eyes on. A huge, deep, round hole in the earth stared into our grief-stricken faces. Evidently, the Russians dug up the bodies after the war – the guide couldn't tell us what happened to the bodies – and left this like a gigantic scar for the world to see.

It pained me so much that I felt my heart go numb and my body freeze from the inside out. Countless faces of people I'd known and who'd lost their lives here arose in my memory. I thought of a distant relative of ours who got buried alive in this pit and managed to escape. His name is now Dr. William Good, and he lives in California. I believe he still practices medicine at the time of this writing. We used to get together with him when we visited Naomi. But there were so, so many more that didn't survive.

At the edge of the giant hole stood a tiny hut that contained a small exhibit of pictures and memorabilia from the Vilno Ghetto. Without saying a word, our guide led Edith and me through the little building and then drove us back to the hotel in the city.

Later that afternoon, Edith and I pulled ourselves together and ventured out again. The Singer House drew us like a magnet. We wanted to find our apartment, but couldn't. At some point they had widened the street and demolished part of the building.

"They must have taken the wing with our apartment off," Edith kept saying, over and over again. That didn't make sense to me because I could still see that part of the house. But the entrance was gone. Eventually, we managed to find Aunt Ella's apartment. A small hotel was there now. It was charming, but empty. The manager, a Lithuanian lady, sat at the desk.

"Can I help you?" she said with a thick accent.

When we told her that we were born in this house and had lived here before the war, she seemed to feel sorry for us. I told her that we couldn't find our apartment. She explained that the old staircase to that part of the house was gone, but that there was another staircase in the back.

"Come on Monday morning, and use the other entrance. The office in your apartment will be open. Just walk in."

We were very grateful and told her so. I knew that if I could see my apartment, it would make this trip for me. But first, according to the original plan we had worked out with our travel agent in the States, the guide and a driver were to take us to Gleboki in Belarus.

We packed food and left very early Sunday morning. The sky was overcast, but it didn't rain, and the ride was comfortable until we came to the border. The Belarusian police took our passports and checked them for two long hours. Finally they let us through. The road changed to cobblestone and, even though the driver slowed down considerably, the ride became bumpy and shaky. After a few hours, we came close to Gleboki. The driver stopped the car, pulled over, and both men guided us on a narrow trail into the forest. It brought back memories of the forest we'd lived in. I didn't like the idea of going into the wilderness with these men and actually got frightened for a moment. But soon we arrived at a meadow and the tour guide unfolded two blankets and unwrapped the food. In the States, we wouldn't dream of having a picnic on a cool, overcast day like this. This was a different world from what Edith and I were used to now, yet it all felt strangely familiar.

Once we entered Gleboki, our guide asked me about the local churches.

"There used to be two churches here, one Roman-Catholic, the other Greek-Orthodox," I said.

"Let's go to the Catholic church," he replied.

Just as we got there, the church bells rang and a large crowd of people streamed out of the church. We were reminded that it was Sunday after all. It took our guide but a moment to pick a man to talk to. They spoke

Russian, and I heard our guide tell the Belarusian that we came from America for a day to see the Jewish ghetto and the mass grave. The man looked us over quickly, and then, without any further hesitation, took us to a local Jewish man named Yasha, which in Yiddish would be Yankel.

Yasha was a shoemaker and lived in a small house, but to him it was luxurious. His voice rang with pride when he showed us his outhouse and said, "See what I made here." He had put in electricity! It seemed to me that he thought we had outhouses in America, too. I didn't tell him differently.

After showing us his tiny home, Yasha and the Belarusian took us around. We saw where the ghetto used to be, and where we lived before there was a ghetto. I wanted to see the school I attended. The old stone building looked so much smaller than I remembered it.

Then they guided us to the mass grave where our grandparents and Uncle Mula were buried. If my parents hadn't gotten the rest of our family to escape before the annihilation of the ghetto, we all would be buried there, too. It was strange to see pretty flowers planted there now, donated by the Jewish community from abroad. There were no remnants of the pits left here, unlike in Ponary, and we couldn't quite make out where the actual grave was situated. Close by, we saw a monument for the Russian prisoners of war who were shot in Gleboki. I still remember the sound of the relentless gunfire in the distance while working in the jam factory, not knowing what would happen to me and my family next.

We also asked them to take us to Uncle Moshe's house, where we lived after the liberation. It was such a shock when we got to the empty lot; Yasha had not warned us. The house had been demolished by the government and something else was to be built instead, we were told, but nothing happened. It was sad to look at the bare piece of land which I remembered so full of life.

Then Yasha took us to the old Jewish cemetery which had been completely destroyed; the local people had taken out the stones for themselves. I don't exactly know what they did with them, but it was a terrible thing to do. Yasha asked for a donation to help restore it. I didn't have much money, but I gave him what I had.

Toward the end of our visit, Yasha invited us to stay for supper. The Russian people are very hospitable and I was curious to see what they ate. Yasha opened some canned fish, and his wife served us blini.

He also opened condensed milk from a can. I think being a shoemaker, he probably often got paid with food. In any case, it seemed that food was no problem here. We thanked our hosts and traveled back during the night hours to our hotel in Vilno. It had been a full day. And even though it brought back many sad memories, it felt good to me to get in touch with my past.

Monday morning we returned with our guide to the Singer House. We walked around the back to where the Lithuanian woman had directed us, and finally found the new entrance.

And then, suddenly, after all this time, there we were. Fifty-five years after walking down the staircase where I said, "Good bye, house, I hope to see you again," we walked these same stairs back up. I get goose bumps even now as I write about it. Edith had tears in her eyes.

Seeing the apartment that we remembered so fondly was difficult. The beautiful shiny black furniture in the dining room was replaced by austere office furniture, just like in our grandparents' apartment. The red shiny floor was neglected and dirty. The mirrors and drapes were gone. We walked from room to room, found the room we had shared, found our parents' bedroom, and eventually found the kitchen. It all looked very different and much smaller than we remembered it. People were working there now, and a young engineer spoke a little English and struck up a conversation with us. When he heard our name was Singer, he was impressed. This wasn't the first time someone reacted this way when he learned our name. There was a senator in the Lithuanian administration now by the name of Singer, the only Jew in the government, but no relation of ours as far as we knew. People seemed to admire Senator Singer and associate us with him.

Before long, we returned to the hotel and, filled with many thoughts and emotions, packed our bags.

The sun peeked through the clouds for once when we left Vilnius with its pretty cathedral, lovely parks, and our River Vilia. They call it Neris now. It is still a beautiful city, and it was very good for me to see it again. It did something for my soul words cannot describe. I often think about it and I am grateful to Al for suggesting the journey.

Chapter Nineteen

We returned to New York on a gorgeous October day. As soon as I stepped out of the airport, I took off my warm raincoat, put on my leather jacket, and felt good. The problem was Al did not feel good.

He had stayed the two weeks with Naomi and was visibly happy to see me. But he had increasing difficulties breathing, so a few days later, we went to Sloan Kettering to see the oncologist. He examined Al and immediately sent him to the hospital to have fluid removed from his lungs. Of course, I stayed with him. Al was discharged home just before Thanksgiving, which we spent at Bobby's house. I treasure the pictures we took of Al with Bobby, Al with Naomi, and of Al with the grandchildren. It was our last Thanksgiving together. There's also a newspaper clipping with a picture from a Christmas musical evening in a private home – taken of him and other Peekskill people in early December of 1994 – that remains a sad memento from those days. When I look at it I can see that even then he still hoped he would conquer the cancer. He didn't even appear to be sick in the picture.

However, the chemo just did not work. Before long he was hospitalized again at Sloan Kettering. I pulled one of the oncologists aside.

"Do you think natural medicine could help my husband? Some people believe in it," I said.

His face looked grave. "We can't help him, and they cannot help him either," he said.

But they did try one other type of injection. Instead of getting relief, Al felt worse. Finally, he told the doctors he didn't want to take them anymore, and they discontinued the injections and suggested for Al to go home and be treated at the local hospital as needed. We got in touch with an oncologist who had trained at Sloan Kettering and was on staff in Mount Kisco. He agreed to treat Al. Then Al collapsed at home. The neighbors suggested I call the ambulance, which took him to the emergency room at the Hudson Valley Hospital Center. From there we called his doctor who had Al transported to the Northern Westchester Hospital in Mount Kisco. I went with him in the ambulance. Even after all these years, when I see an ambulance, I sometimes wonder, if inside a wife, mustering up all her courage in order not to feel and show her fear, is holding the hand of her deathly ill husband who's struggling for each breath.

In Mount Kisco, he was operated on again and much fluid was removed from his lungs. After the surgery, he seemed to feel somewhat better; his breathing definitely eased. Next he developed terrible hiccups. The oncologist gave him medication for it and Al experienced some relief. He wasn't conscious most of the time, but he recognized us all. The children came to his bedside every evening. His close friends stopped by to show their support. I spent every day with him in the hospital from morning until night, often leaving the house before it was light out and getting home when it was pitch dark, as it was December and the days were short. Edith had a bad flu and couldn't travel, so her husband, Amos, came from Chicago to stay with me and drive with me on the snowy country roads to and from the hospital. I remember the beautiful, cheery Christmas decorations in the town of Mount Kisco and in the hospital while it was the saddest time of my life.

One day, the oncologist asked to talk to the children and me in private, outside of Al's room. Naomi, Bobby, Sherri, and I met with him.

"Al is not going to come out alive from this hospital," he said.

It was very hard to hear this. Even though we somehow expected it, we were stunned.

I got a private nurse to stay with Al at night, but it didn't help much. Edith had recovered from the flu and came to stay with me while Amos went back to Chicago. Finally, I decided to take Al home. There was nothing they could do for him in the hospital and they had started talking about transferring him to hospice or discharging him home. They brought a hospital bed and Al stayed right in the room where I am writing these words now.

A social worker and a nurse from hospice stopped by frequently. I also hired a nurses' aide from the agency. At night she slept on the couch next to Al, so that I could get some rest in our bedroom. But I hardly slept at all. I remember getting up and watching him while she slept peacefully next to her patient. I also stayed by his bedside all day, every day.

Edith remained with me for another week and left. The children and grandchildren visited all the time. We couldn't know how much longer this would last.

Whenever the social worker from hospice came, she told me that he would die soon. It was debilitating to me. Every time she left I had a headache. Two days after Christmas, the hospice nurse came to check on Al.

"He is dying and you should make funeral arrangements," she said.

"As long as he is alive, there is hope," I answered.

She called the hospital social worker and complained that I didn't accept that my husband was dying. When she hung up the phone, I told her to call the Jewish Center. She did, and she spoke to the Rabbi. He knew that Al was sick and came to the house immediately. So did the social worker, Fran Feldman, who was a neighbor.

We sat down in the living room to talk. The young Rabbi said that I was right.

"As long as there is life, there is hope," he said.

In the middle of the conversation, the aide came into the living room and called me. We walked into the den where Al was lying in the hospital bed and I immediately knew that he was dead. He was still warm. I kissed him one last time. It all still feels like a bad dream to me.

Even now, writing about the funeral is difficult.

A tremendous number of people attended: family, friends, neighbors, colleagues, his staff including people who had worked for him years ago, and of course countless patients. Even the mayor of Peekskill came. Not only were there not enough seats for everybody – the standing room was overcrowded and people had to wait outside the chapel. The chorus of sniffles and noses being blown seemed constant. Both children spoke about their father with much feeling and pride. So many good words by so many good people were said about my husband. I remember one of Al's colleagues, calling him "the American success story." The newspaper wrote about Al as "a man for all seasons." For months, I received letters from his patients and other people whose lives Al had touched, filled with descriptions of how wonderful he was.

One of the most horrific experiences of my entire lifetime was to watch how they put him into the ground. Even though, intellectually, I knew he had died, and even though his death was hardly a surprise given the severity and length of his illness and how weak he'd gotten and how much he'd suffered, the hard reality of seeing the casket being lowered into the ground hit me in a way I cannot relate in words. How could this young man, only sixty-nine years old, so full of life, be put into the ground forever?

The Shiva provided a brief respite for me. It is a seven-day period when the family of the deceased mourns him and people come to pay respects. It is a wonderful custom. I didn't have the time to think or worry about anything. Hordes of people came and went constantly, from early morning till late at night. The amount of food I received was unbelievable. Any kind of food you could possibly imagine, loads of cakes, whole dinners from Colonial Terrace. There was so much food that I had to give some away. One of the young girls who'd helped me while Al was sick remembered that I liked vegetable lasagna and made it for me. I was very moved and grateful for all this kindness.

And then I was alone.

It was wintertime, early January of 1995. Usually we went to Florida in the winter, but that season, of course, we couldn't. Our friends from Florida kept calling me and asking me to come down and not to stay home alone. But I had a lot of things to take care of. I ended up remaining in Peekskill for thirty days until I had completed most of the important paperwork like social security and that sort of thing. Interestingly enough, staying home for thirty days after a loved one's death is a Jewish custom, but I didn't do it on purpose; it just worked out that way. The children continued helping me a lot and, together with my friends, they convinced me to spend some time in Florida after all.

But despite the change of scenery, the sadness stayed the same. It was like a physical pain – I felt the loss in my whole body. I remember not long after I arrived in Florida, at a friend's house, a woman asked me where my husband was. She blushed when I told her, "He passed away," and I fought hard to hold back my tears.

Things didn't get easier for a long time. The entire first year was like a nightmare. And that's with wonderful children and friends taking care of me. What it must be like for people who don't have the support system I have, I cannot imagine.

Chapter Twenty

AFTER A VERY DIFFICULT MONTH in Florida I returned to Peekskill. Here I was lonely, too. I forced myself to go to Hadassah meetings, but there wasn't any joy in it anymore for me for quite some time. My friend, Emilia – the poet with the much younger husband, Victor, from whom I'd taken piano lessons and with whom we'd traveled to Italy – called me frequently and invited me to go out. Sometimes I did, sometimes I didn't. She tried to convince me to go to the Hospital Ball with them, as Al and I had done every year. I just knew I'd be miserable, feeling the tremendous void where Al had been all night. So I didn't go.

Elsa, another artistic friend of mine, also went out of her way to try and cheer me up. Elsa was a German voice teacher. She and her husband had been patients of Al's. She was also acquainted with our neighbor and friend, Eddie; they volunteered together at the Paramount Art Center in Peekskill. Her husband, Santo Alberti, was Italian-American and had met Elsa when he was a GI in Germany. He now owned a store in Peekskill that dealt in alarms and musical equipment and, together with Elsa, he hosted many lovely musical gatherings at the store. So she got me out to those events, as well as to shows including a ballet at the Paramount. It was good for me and, little by little, I began enjoying social and cultural activities again.

Before Al's first Yahrzeit[9], my nephrologist told me that my kidneys were failing and that I needed to have a graft put in to be ready for dialysis. It was very painful. My arm was red and swollen for a long time.

---

9 Anniversary of the death of a close relative

In the meantime, I was able to stay away from dialysis for two more years, thanks to Epogen injections and diet.

In the late spring of 1997, Emilia called and asked me to meet her and Victor for lunch in Yorktown, which was not unusual. What was unusual was that when I came to the restaurant, a man was sitting with the two of them. Everybody got up and Emilia looked at me attentively.

"This is our friend Glen, an artist. He and his wife were good friends of ours," she said.

Glen's wife had died the year before. By now Al had been gone over two years. At the end of the lunch, Glen invited me to WestPoint to a show and I agreed to go and had a good time.

Emilia was getting old, her heart was failing, but she was sharp as ever. Edith happened to be visiting me when Emilia celebrated her 90th birthday. For the occasion, I invited Emilia, Victor, Glen, and Edith to a lovely restaurant on the Hudson. It could have been a beautiful outing, if not for Glen who was quiet, had a dark expression on his face, and was almost abrupt with me.

Emilia took me aside. "He's just in one of his moods," she said.

A little later, I saw her talk to him which seemed to me like she was trying to straighten him out. But I lost interest.

Soon afterwards, I visited Edith in Chicago and later in the summer I'd planned to go on a cruise to Alaska with a couple from Florida. But when I arrived in Seattle, where I had to change planes to get to Vancouver, my legs were so swollen that I couldn't walk. They had to put me in a wheelchair. I barely made it to the hotel room in Vancouver and immediately called Naomi. She advised me to order room service, take some Tylenol, and reassess the situation in the morning. I slept all night and very much to my surprise was able to walk again the next day. I skipped the city tour, but I didn't have to miss out on seeing Alaska after all. It turned out to be a beautiful cruise.

Shortly after I returned to Peekskill, Emilia called me to make a lunch date. She had an appointment with her cardiologist and we agreed to meet at the Chinese restaurant nearby. When I arrived at the restaurant, Glen was waiting for me. He made no secret of being overjoyed to see me. From then on, Glen and I got together often. He still had a subscription to West Point for two and every weekend he drove all the way from Garrison to pick me up and to take me home. It was more than an hour extra driving for him each way. Soon I gave up my subscription. And we often met for lunch or dinner with Emilia and Victor. In the beginning, more than anything we had the love for the arts in common, but over time I came to value him as a very good man.

Glen grew up in Indiana and was raised Presbyterian during his early childhood. His mother came from an old Southern family. His father was of Swedish origin.

"He was a policeman, and he was very strict," Glen told me.

Glen's father died when Glen was nine years old. His mother married a Baptist and changed religion. Glen didn't like his stepfather and became estranged from his mother. He became disillusioned with religion and, before he turned eighteen, he joined the Navy. I can still see the photograph of the handsome seventeen-year-old boy from Indiana in my mind's eye. He served on a ship that was hit by friendly fire, by another American boat. Glen got amnesia and for months couldn't even remember his own name. This is a story he liked to tell over and over again.

Glen married young, they had a daughter, but they got divorced soon thereafter. He traveled for a while until he got to New York. He'd always liked to paint, so he went to art school in Manhattan. Here he fell in love with a pretty Jewish girl who had a beautiful voice. Amy came from Pleasantville and after they got married, they moved to Westchester.

"Her father was liberal and liked me," Glen said, "but her mother never did."

Over time it became clear to me that Glen and his wife were free spirits. They did not practice any religion, but were good people, very charitable and helpful to others, which is much more important to me than anything else.

In confidence, Emilia told me a story that showed me that Glen and I had something else in common.

After several years of trying to have children, Glen and Amy adopted a boy and a girl. A few years later, Amy became pregnant after all and gave birth to another boy. One day, Amy put too much paper in the fire place and the house went up in flames. The older boy didn't realize that Amy had taken the baby outside with her and ran back into the burning house to rescue his little brother. When Glen returned home from his work as a designer in the city, he found his house gone and his older son dead.

"Glen's hair turned gray overnight from grief," Emilia concluded the tragic story with a deep sigh. I felt much empathy for Glen, having lost a child myself, but we never talked about the loss of our sons. I don't even think I ever told Emilia about Pipsi.

In the winter of 1997 my doctor sent me to the emergency room. I felt terribly weak and short of breath. When they checked my blood, they found that the creatinine and BUN were sky high. My kidneys were failing. No wonder I felt like I was dying.

The graft that caused me so much pain when it was put in had closed by then and was completely useless. The surgeon put a temporary graft in my chest, which once again was very painful, and they started dialysis immediately. I was hospitalized for two weeks in Phelps Memorial Hospital in Tarrytown, where they inserted yet another graft, this time into my right arm and, even when I got discharged home, I was still very sick.

The day after my release from the hospital I started the regimen of dialysis three times a week. The dialysis clinic was in Carmel, a twenty-minute-drive from us. However, they didn't have a spot during the day available, and it took the patient transportation bus almost two hours on the snowy country roads. So I never got home till late at night when it was pitch dark and freezing cold. On New Year's Eve, Naomi picked me up and brought me to her house for the holiday. I was weak and could not stay home alone. Edith came and took care of me for a little while, but she had to go back to work and attend to the needs of her family. So I called an agency for help. They sent Margaret, who worked for me for over a year. In the meantime a dialysis clinic was opened locally. What a relief it was when we didn't have to drive that far in the dark of the night anymore. I went to dialysis three times a week. Four days I was free to live a normal life.

When I asked my nephrologist about traveling to Florida, he gave his permission and the social worker in the clinic found me a dialysis clinic in South Florida. Margaret, however, only agreed to go for a month, so we went in March. Margaret took a big wardrobe with her, and in Florida she went shopping like mad. She bought so much, she had to ship it back home. Margaret ended up loving Florida.

Not that a dialysis clinic is ever a very pleasant place, but the one I went to in Florida was particularly unpleasant. The doctors were curt and the nurses unfriendly. There was nothing I could do about it though; I needed to go there three times a week to stay alive.

March of 1997 was unseasonably hot and humid. So when our air conditioning broke down in the condo, we had to wait several days until a repairman was available to fix it. In the meantime I slept on the screened-in terrace. It was lovely to sleep outdoors in the balmy night air. It reminded me of our early summers in New York when we first came to the United States.

Palm Aire, the development where our condo is located, is picturesque with tall olive trees and a wide variety of palms. There's much birdsong during the day and a constant cricket concert once the sun has set. Across from our building flows a canal on whose banks I love to go for walks. It's reminiscent of the Vilia River in Vilno, and Edith and I sometimes joke and call the bridge closest to us the Green Bridge. During that month, I went swimming in our development's heated pool on all days I was off dialysis. It gave me such a sense of wellbeing. And I got to socialize with many old friends and go to the opera and see a show at the Caldwell Theater. Despite the difficulties at the dialysis clinic, it was the first stay in Florida I genuinely enjoyed since Al had died.

When I first went on dialysis, I hardly saw my friends at all. Later, when I went to dialysis here in Cortlandt, I was able to resume my social life and by now I had a comfortable routine.

Three days a week, I went to dialysis from 11:00 a.m. till 2:00 p.m. It took another hour to be taken off. I was always very, very tired afterwards. Margaret would bring me home, had dinner ready for me and, as soon as I ate, I'd lie down for the rest of the day. Four days a week I lived a normal life. Glen and I met every weekend and went to concerts or to the movies or to restaurants together. I very much appreciated that he stayed with me even when I went on dialysis. Many men would not have been as understanding and would have gotten scared around a woman with such severe medical problems. But, once again, life didn't stay carefree for long.

Emilia had another heart attack and was taken to the hospital. This time she didn't come out. Her death was such an immense loss to me.

"She knew that she was going to die," Victor told me later, in tears.

"You have family, you are not alone. Keep in touch with them," she'd said to him on the way to the hospital. Emilia and Victor did not have children together. She was talking about her children and grandchildren from her first marriage.

I remember going to her wake and to church before dialysis. Glen came too. I shared my grief with him.

"I lost too many people I loved lately," I said. "First my mother, then my husband, now my friend. I'll miss her so much."

Glen listened and remained a good friend to me even though I was sad a lot.

The next winter, I made my own arrangements for dialysis in Florida. A neighbor in Palm Aire had told me about another clinic, closer to me, in Fort Lauderdale. It turned out to be better, except that in the beginning, I came home and suffered terrible pain. They probably set it too high. Later they adjusted it and I felt better. But I never complained. I was glad to be in Florida. Edith stayed with me a few weeks which was a big help. I got a girl from the agency a few times a week to drive me to dialysis and to make me something to eat.

That year, Glen took a trip across America. He drove to Indiana to visit his family whom he had not seen since he came to New York and got married. He hadn't kept in touch with them and didn't know how they would receive him. I found that so difficult to understand – how can you have family that's alive and not have any contact with them for thirty years?

Fortunately, they were happy to see him. From there he drove to New Orleans to see his son, who was studying law there. Then he drove to Florida to visit with me. The pictures he showed me were a testimony that he'd had a joyful reunion with his loved ones.

Glen and I had a good time together and he met some of my friends. It was a pleasant winter for me. I went for a walk by the canal in the morning before dialysis and went swimming on the days when I was off dialysis.

When I came home in April, Naomi found me a caretaker whom a friend of hers had recommended. Cecille was Jamaican. She stayed with me, drove me to dialysis, and cooked spicy food which I did not like.

One day, just before my birthday in 1999, when I was in dialysis, a nurse called out to me from the nurses' station.

"Somebody is calling you from the Medical Center in Valhalla. You probably don't want to take it now," she said.

"I'll take it," I replied.

The voice on the other end said, "This is the Transplant Center. We have a kidney. It may be a match for you. Come over and we'll test you again."

My hands trembled. "I can come after dialysis."

"So be here at 6:00 p.m."

Immediately, I called Naomi who called Bobby. Cecille drove me to the Medical Center in Valhalla where the children and my daughter-in-law Sherri met me. The additional tests confirmed that it was a match. It meant I could go for the transplant operation. Naomi cried when the doctor had difficulties finding a vein to give me anesthesia. She asked me to reconsider and not have the operation.

But I was sure that I wanted to go through with it. I wanted a kidney that worked, so I just had to take the chance. It was the best decision I ever made. I am still alive because of it.

Soon afterwards they transported me to the operating room. The surgery took six hours. I stayed in the recovery room for twenty-four hours. When they wheeled me to my room I felt as if I'd been run over by a truck. But it was the best birthday present I ever received. I was seventy-three years old and got a new lease on life.

It took a few days until we knew that my body did not reject the new kidney. I was given many medications, including morphine intravenously for pain, and steroids which caused diabetes as a side effect. In addition to the diabetes, I developed bad stomach pain. The tests showed a fungus in my intestines. They gave me another medicine for it and it was taken care of. The diabetes presented more of a problem. At the same, time I was exceedingly happy to have a working kidney. It was a gift of life. I was very grateful to the person who donated the kidney. I never found out who the donor was, but I wrote a thank you letter to the family. They didn't reply.

Naomi visited every day. Bobby, who always worked late in his law firm, came in the evenings as well. As soon as I could get out of bed, I got up for meals and walked a little. Glen came to visit, and many friends and neighbors called. After two weeks, the social worker started making arrangements for me to go to rehab. My nephrologist, Dr. Delaney didn't want me to go home alone. I still had to learn how to give myself insulin injections for the diabetes. But I was anxious to get out of the hospital. It was summer and my roses were in bloom. I knew that I would recuperate much better in my own environment than in any rehab. So I convinced the doctor that I had plenty of help, including a live-in health care aide, and she finally wrote the discharge papers.

Initially, all went well. A visiting nurse came to give me insulin injections and teach me how to prepare my meds for a week. Edith came for a week from Chicago which was a tremendous help. She went food shopping with Cecille and cooked meals that agreed with me.

As soon as Edith left, Cecille told me that she was going to Jamaica for a week. I was in no condition to stay alone in the house, so she promised to ask a friend to take care of me. This woman came once. When I asked her to do something for me, she said that she had to go shopping and walked out. When she had not returned a few hours later, I got worried and called her house. Somebody told me that she quit and wouldn't come back.

This happened on a weekend. The agency was closed until Monday. I was alone after a serious operation and could not get help. Finally I called a neighbor of Cecille's. She told me that she worked nights, but could come for a few hours during the day. Unfortunately she did not drive. I had a doctor's appointment, so I drove the two of us.

When Cecille returned the following week, I told her what her friend had done to me. Cecille didn't say much and was her usual carefree self. The other problem with her was that she didn't keep the house clean, which annoyed me to no end.

So I called a cleaning service I used to know. The owner, a Polish woman by the name of Danuta, sent two girls who cleaned my house meticulously. I spoke Polish to the girls and asked if they happened to know somebody who could help me. A few days later, Danuta called me and told me that her sister-in-law just arrived from Poland and needed a job. We set up an appointment and met. The language was no problem for me. I hired Grazyna in August of 1999 and she is still with me at the time of this writing, in 2010. She went to Poland a few times, but always came back. She worked hard all these years, even took on extra jobs on the weekends, to pay for her daughter's education in Poland and help out her mother. I always respected that and still do.

Finally, some stability seemed to return to my life. Before long I didn't need the insulin injections anymore. Not to be tied to a three-times-a-week dialysis schedule felt like liberation from slavery, and not to fear death from kidney failure truly was a gift of life. I once wrote a short story about this and called it "A Survivor Again." To be able to urinate and eat an orange was heaven. Even now, almost every time I go to the bathroom, I thank God. We take it for granted, but it is an extraordinary function.

Two pleasant years went by. One Sunday, I waited for Glen to pick me up to go to West Point for a show. We had an argument – I don't even remember what it was about – and had not seen each other the previous weekend. I was annoyed when he was late, but when it became clear that he actually wasn't going to show, I felt angry and upset.

"I can't believe I'm being stood up," I thought to myself. There was no way I was going to sit around the house by myself – it was the weekend and Grazyna was out – so I put on my coat, got into my car, and went to the movies alone.

The first thing I looked at when I returned home was the answering machine. The light wasn't blinking. Finally, I decided to call him. His answering machine went on.

"Strange," I thought. Where was he? I left another message before I went to bed.

Two days later, on Tuesday morning, his daughter-in-law called me and said that they found Glen dead in his house on Monday. He'd been dead for a few days. She briefly informed me that his memorial would be at the art gallery in Garrison.

Stunned, I hung up the phone and sat down at the kitchen table. I thought back to the last time we saw each other, two weeks earlier, and suddenly I remembered something he'd shared with me. He was completely okay, there was no sign of any illness whatsoever, but he told me that he had been thinking and that he had called his son to tell him that he wanted to be cremated.

I asked a Hadassah friend to come with me to the memorial service. She drove and I gave a speech about his life and I was later told it carried the whole ceremony. One of his friends described him as an "American original." Indeed, he was different from many American men. He did not care for ball games, but he liked classical music and, of course, he was an artist and loved art.

I remember Glen fondly. He was reserved and a good person, and he came into my life when I needed a friend. He was enjoyable company and we got along well for the most part. We had a lot in common. So I was very sad after Glen died. I went for Thanksgiving to Bobby's in New York. It was comforting to be with family and especially with my delightful grandchildren.

After Thanksgiving I went to Florida for the winter. It was wonderful not to go to dialysis anymore. I still missed Glen and just wanted to relax. I had absolutely no interest in meeting other men. Once again life had something else in store for me.

He was tall and handsome and a smooth liar. I was honest and true as usual. At the age of seventy-four, I was swept off my feet like a teenager, and I was hurt deeply. It took me a long time to get over it. In the spring, I went back home and was happy to spend time with my children and grandchildren. This is always healing.

A couple of years later, I went to the First Hebrew Congregation for a lecture held by the Rabbi. Eddie was there, our neighbor and friend who had volunteered at the Paramount together with other friends of mine. After the lecture he came over and talked with me. Over refreshments he told me that his girlfriend had broken up with him. A few days later he called me and we started getting together frequently.

There was a certain ease and comfort between us that comes with having been friends for years. I knew him well and we had a lot in common. Even though he was getting old, he remained outgoing and still had many lady friends. He used to say that his male friends died, but his lady friends were alive. During the day he had a caretaker but in the evenings he couldn't stay home. So we often went out – to the diner or other local restaurants, also to the movies and to the Paramount Center which he helped to restore years ago. New people ran it now but, any time we went there, several people struck up a conversation with Eddie and commented on how much he had contributed to the Paramount. My children liked him as well. Bobby and Sherri especially enjoyed Eddie's lively company.

One night, in the summer of 2007, I suddenly felt a severe pain in my chest, radiating to my left shoulder and arm. Instantly, I knew it was from my heart. Luckily, Grazyna was home. I woke her up and she drove me to the emergency room.

An emergency doctor took care of me right away, and even though it was night, my family physician soon showed up and then my cardiologist came for a while. I was having a mild heart attack. They kept me in the emergency room overnight. In the morning I called Naomi and she was by my side in no time. She called Bobby who also came immediately. I stayed in the hospital a few days. Eddie visited me and other friends came to see me as well. I especially remember Arlene, Selda, and Thelma. When I was discharged, the hospital arranged for a visiting nurse and a physical therapist to come to the house for a while. Shortly after my discharge home, Edith invited me to her granddaughter's Bat Mitzvah. I knew that I would be able to relax at my sister's house, so off I went to Chicago. Even though my cardiologist didn't want me to travel, I stayed there for two weeks. It was good for me and my heart.

When I returned home, I continued to see Eddie. He was lonely just like I was. When he was young, he had many friends, but not anymore. Before long he lost his caretaker; she moved to Georgia. His children did not want him to drive at night. So he started talking about moving to an assisted living facility. He found one close by and asked me to move there, too. But I was not ready for this way of life and I'm still not.

After living in the overcrowded ghetto with over ten people in one room, sharing our space with many people in the bunker in the woods, followed by several more years in crammed quarters after the war, I savor having my own house and my privacy. It's not luxurious, but it's comfortable and filled with a multitude of memories. Sometimes I can still hear the children's laughter when they were growing up. I love my collection of souvenirs from all over the world, and pretty much everything I touch in this house has a story. And there's a peacefulness and quiet here that I never found anywhere else. So I went to visit Eddie many times, but I had absolutely no interest in moving there.

Not much later, I went to Florida for the winter as usual. Eddie and I spoke on the phone a few times. He seemed well and sounded like he had made friends, which was no surprise to me. When I came home in the spring, I was busy catching up with things. That evening I read in the local paper that the home where he lived was being closed and the people were being transferred somewhere else. I called him, but did not get an answer. The next day his daughter called me to tell me that Eddie died and the funeral was the following day.

I went with my neighbors. His children had arranged a military funeral which was attended by many people. Since Eddie was not religious, there was no Shiva. Not that we were that religious, but I remember when Al died, sitting Shiva for seven days was most helpful and even healing to me. I find it one of the most sensible customs in the Jewish tradition.

I had lost another friend. More and more of my contemporaries were dying or getting sick. And another health issue that affected me at least as much as the kidney failure got progressively worse. Only it was never life threatening.

My eyesight was always excellent. Not until I went back to school in my mid-forties did I require reading glasses. I found this to be such a nuisance in the beginning, but after a while I got used to it. One year – I don't remember when exactly, Al was still alive – my ophthalmologist told me that I had macular degeneration.

"Don't worry about it," he assured me. "You have the dry type, which is harmless." So I didn't give it much thought.

My eyesight worsened considerably after the kidney transplant, and I was told I had developed cataracts, a side effect from the steroids. I consulted several ophthalmologists and eye surgeons, and the opinions whether to operate on the cataracts with the underlying macular degeneration varied widely. In the end, I went with the doctors who recommended the surgery. For a short while my vision improved. Then it deteriorated again, and I received disheartening news: there was blood in my left eye now. My macular degeneration had become the wet type, the dangerous type.

To make a very long story short, after seeing more ophthalmologists, retinologists, and eye surgeons than I ever saw kidney doctors, and after undergoing several procedures including laser surgery and excruciating injections directly into the eyeball, I was left legally blind in my left eye. However, Dr. Slakter in New York City and Dr. Rosenfeld in Florida were able to save my right eye and keep me from going entirely blind. Dr. Slakter is not only an excellent physician, he also has a wonderful way with his patients, similar to Al. I still see both doctors regularly, and my eyes have been stable for a couple of years now.

It was extremely difficult to get used to poor vision. The hardest part was not being able to read books and magazines and having to depend on others to drive me around. It was a gradual process and, thankfully, I can still write and take care of my bills with a powerful magnifying glass. Sherri, my daughter-in-law, supplies me with recordings of excellent books. I'm able to enjoy the movies and the theater, but my eyes are very, very sensitive. They hurt and itch much of the time; sunglasses and eye drops are my constant companions these days. When Grazyna is not around on the weekends, I still occasionally drive myself to the beauty parlor or to the movie theater during daylight hours. I suspect my children will give me grief when they read this, but that's life.

Chapter Twenty-One

It is late April of 2010, and another season in Florida is coming to an end. Grazyna and I have started our annual routine of packing, and I'm looking forward to returning to my home on Birchwood Lane. Spring is in full force here, and I know it's even more beautiful up north. When Naomi came down to visit recently, I had bronchitis. Instead of going out and doing fun things, I needed to rest and she took care of me. My body is taking any cold or virus much harder than it used to, and recovery takes longer. Everything is more tiring than it used to be, and I spend much of my time in doctors' offices. For the most part, I go with the flow but sometimes it frustrates me.

I'm very happy that, along with the completion of this season, comes the completion of this manuscript. Both Al and I never wanted to speak about our past. Al especially completely blocked it out. I didn't want to spend too much time in the past either. We wanted to move forward, make a new life for ourselves and for our children. We didn't want to expose our children to the horrors we experienced, didn't want them to hate other people but rather wanted them to love everybody. Both Al and I felt people were just people. Many of Al's patients were Germans and felt comfortable with him. Naomi's childhood friend from across the street is German and they are still close.

Not until I went back to school did I begin talking about what happened to us. One teacher in particular kept asking me about my experiences. Even then I kept my answers to a minimum. Now in my old age, however, writing down my life story has been tremendously meaningful and healing for me.

Less than a handful of the family members who survived in the

Alice Singer-Genis with Emunah Herzog

woods together are still alive today: Cousin Aryeh, Cousin Asya, Edith, and I. Aryeh and Asya both live in Israel.

Asya and I speak on the phone regularly. She too has many health problems. Her mother, Aunt Ella, died in 1979 of heart disease, after Asya took care of her for five years in her home. Asya has two daughters, several grandchildren, and she's the first of our generation to have a great-grandchild.

Unfortunately, I'm not able to talk with Aryeh much. He had a stroke in his forties and nowadays speaks Hebrew only. I'm told even that is hard to understand. His wife, Rina, speaks English, so we talk on the phone occasionally. They have two sons and a daughter. Aryeh sounds cheerful, though, and took up painting some years ago. Last time we visited Israel, I looked at hundreds of his paintings. They are incredibly colorful, and many of them have been exhibited and are truly excellent. Almost all deal with the Holocaust in some way. Aryeh stayed in the Israeli Army Reserve until he had the stroke. He became a civil engineer and, to this day, he goes to the office every day. His daughter runs it now.

His mother, Aunt Chaya, remarried and gave birth to a baby-girl. Miri became a nurse like so many in our family. She was always very helpful to us when we visited Israel, and she still goes out of her way when someone from our family, now the younger generations, travel to Israel. Aunt Chaya died in 2005 at the age of ninety-seven of heart failure in Miri's home.

Aunt Celia died suddenly in 1978 in a head-on collision. Her daughter, Miriam, still lives in Chicago with her family. That leaves Uncle Moshe and Aunt Hannah from our core group in the woods to write about. They stayed in Israel even though their son Elliot made his home in Chicago with his wife Doris, also a survivor. Elliot has children and grandchildren, and he and Doris spend their winters in Boca Raton. Uncle Moshe died in 1974 of a heart attack. Aunt Hannah never recovered from this loss. In a way, she died with him and only went through the motions for the rest of her life. Eventually, she moved into a nursing home and passed in 1983.

When I look back on my life, I see how many things I accomplished; yet while I was doing it I never felt it was good enough. From working in a factory and a food store to working in the laboratory at Queens General

Hospital, to getting a B.A. and Masters in psychology and a certification as a school psychologist and working as a school psychologist, to becoming a biofeedback therapist and working as such, at the same time being a mother and wife and working for Hadassah and the community made me a busy woman. I did a lot for Hadassah, but Hadassah did even more for me. It gave meaning to my life.

Sometimes I wonder if I would have been happier if I had worked in my chosen profession. I always regretted not being a physician. Who knows how much my sickness at such a young age had to do with my depression. As the saying goes, "The mind can be a killer, and the mind can be a healer." Yes, losing potassium is a chemical process and medical problem. However, I know that there is a distinct correlation between the mind and the body.

It is likely that had I followed my dream, I would not be included in the "Who is Who in America" and "Who is Who of American Women" and "Who is Who in the East," and likely I would not have been chosen Woman of Merit by Hadassah. Yet I might have been happier. Today I believe one should follow one's heart and one's dreams, a lesson I feel I learned too late in life.

I had many good times. I loved traveling. To meet different people and visit different places was always a thrill. There were many fantastic trips I didn't get to write about. I sometimes wonder when it was that we didn't identify as Europeans any longer and began identifying as Americans.

Psychology still is my love; it helped me so much as a person. Even though I stopped playing the piano when Al died, my love for music and the arts in general never lessened. Aside from our extensive travels, living close to New York City enabled me to experience great opera, ballet, and theater performances. After Al sold the office, we held a subscription at the Metropolitan Opera in the winter as well as a subscription to the ABT (American Ballet Theater) in the spring. Even after Al died, friends frequently picked me up to go to the ballet in the city. And I often went to the Metropolitan Museum in Manhattan when I visited my son. The Hudson Valley always offered a lot culturally, and even Peekskill isn't as provincial and conservative as it used to be. Many artists have moved here, there are nightclubs and restaurants from many corners of the world, the Paramount now hosts world-class shows for all age groups, and the Riverfront is a beautiful area where not a weekend goes by without some kind of event. I am not gardening any longer, but I still enjoy my backyard with the tall, old trees, and I love living in my house even though it's too big for me. It goes without saying that I would much prefer to still have Al by my side.

So when I think about it, there was more good than bad in my life and I'm very grateful. To survive the Second World War and the Holocaust with my family was a blessing. I was lucky enough to get another chance on life by receiving a kidney from a cadaver of a person I did not know. I enjoy my children and grandchildren. Unfortunately, Al died young and could not watch his grandchildren grow up.

To this day, Bobby quotes his father saying, "If you have a roof over your head, food on your table, and nobody is shooting at you, you're a happy person."

It's interesting, Al always was the kind of doctor whose patients came first no matter what. He was a legend. Yet after he died, the young dentist who took over Al's office shared a significant conversation with me.

The young man had asked Al, "What's the secret of your success?"

I was quite surprised when I heard Al's answer.

"Don't worry about this kind of success. You are doing the right thing. You're an excellent father and a very good husband. Family comes first."

It certainly looks like I won't be hungry when I die; I'm not even hungry for meaning anymore, now that I have written down my life story and can see the bigger picture more clearly. Life is not as we plan it and not always as we want it to be. The secret to being happy is to like life more than dislike it, to make the best with what it offers us. I just want to spend the rest of my life peacefully and wish that all generations to come get to live in a peaceful world.

I Won't Die Hungry

My family celebrating Thanksgiving. Bottom row, from left to right: Isaiah, Mariah, me, Brittany, and Ryan. Back row, from left to right: Sherri, Bob, Naomi and Harold.
Scarsdale, New York (2010)

Acknowledgements

I would like to extend my sincere thanks and appreciation to my daughter Naomi and my son Robert for their help with this book. Heartfelt thanks also to my sister, Edith, for her input.

I wish to give special recognition to Alan Adelson from Jewish Heritage and to Emunah Herzog for their assistance and influence, as well as to Eva Feeley for proofreading the manuscript.

I gratefully thank my parents for not only saving my life, but for setting an example of how to live honestly and to be a giving person. Through the darkest of times my parents never compromised their dignity and integrity.

Much love to my husband, Al, a friend and life partner for forty-eight years. Like my parents, the horror he experienced did not harden him. Instead, it made him more resolute in his desire to reach out to others through his profession. From his days as a young, fearless partisan, as a dedicated student, as a beloved family man and a dentist, he never ceased to be my hero and my rock.

My thoughts go to my grandparents, aunt, uncles, cousins, and friends who perished in the Holocaust.

I am deeply grateful to all people who helped us to survive the horrors of the war and the Holocaust.

Alice Singer-Genis